About Access Archaeology

Access Archaeology offers a different publishing model for specialist academic material that might traditionally prove commercially unviable, perhaps due to its sheer extent or volume of colour content, or simply due to its relatively niche field of interest.

All *Access Archaeology* publications are available in open-access e-pdf format and in (on-demand) print format. The open-access model supports dissemination in areas of the world where budgets are more severely limited, and also allows individual academics from all over the world the chance to access the material privately, rather than relying solely on their university or public library. Print copies, nevertheless, remain available to individuals and institutions who need or prefer them.

The material is professionally refereed, but not peer reviewed. Copy-editing takes place prior to submission of the work for publication and is the responsibility of the author. Academics who are able to supply print-ready material are not charged any fee to publish (including making the material available in open-access). In some instances the material is type-set in-house and in these cases a small charge is passed on for layout work.

This model works for us as a publisher because we are able to publish specialist work with relatively little editorial investment. Our core effort goes into promoting the material, both in open-access and print, where *Access Archaeology* books get the same level of attention as our core peer-reviewed imprint by being included in marketing e-alerts, print catalogues, displays at academic conferences and more, supported by professional distribution worldwide.

Open-access allows for greater dissemination of the academic work than traditional print models, even lithographic printing, could ever hope to support. It is common for a new open-access e-pdf to be downloaded several hundred times in its first month since appearing on our website. Print sales of such specialist material would take years to match this figure, if indeed it ever would.

By printing 'on-demand', meanwhile, (or, as is generally the case, maintaining minimum stock quantities as small as two), we are able to ensure orders for print copies can be fulfilled without having to invest in great quantities of stock in advance. The quality of such printing has moved forward radically, even in the last few years, vastly increasing the fidelity of images (highly important in archaeology) and making colour printing more economical.

Access Archaeology is a vehicle that allows us to publish useful research, be it a PhD thesis, a catalogue of archaeological material or data, in a model that does not cost more than the income it generates.

This model may well evolve over time, but its ambition will always remain to publish archaeological material that would prove commercially unviable in traditional publishing models, without passing the expense on to the academic (author or reader).

The Classification of Chalcolithic and Early Bronze Age Copper and Bronze Axe-heads from Southern Britain

Stuart Needham

Access Archaeology

Archaeopress Publishing Ltd
Gordon House
276 Banbury Road
Oxford OX2 7ED

www.archaeopress.com

ISBN 978 1 78491 740 1
ISBN 978 1 78491 741 8 (e-Pdf)

© Archaeopress and S Needham 2017

Printed and bound in Great Britain by
Marston Book Services Ltd, Oxfordshire

All rights reserved. No part of this book may be reproduced or transmitted,
in any form or by any means, electronic, mechanical, photocopying or otherwise,
without the prior written permission of the copyright owners.

The Classification of Chalcolithic and Early Bronze Age Copper and Bronze Axe-heads from Southern Britain

The scheme presented below is based on the author's previously unpublished doctoral thesis (Needham 1983)[1] which presented a corpus and full classification of flat, low-flanged and long-flanged axes (strictly axe-heads) of the Chalcolithic and Early Bronze Age for central and southern England. Although some aspects of the classification and some particular types have been defined in past publications, the scheme as a whole has not been presented in published form. The northern boundary of the study area was defined by the Mersey and Humber rivers, the material beyond having already been catalogued by Schmidt & Burgess (1981). Similarly, Wales was excluded because the equivalent material there was due to be published as part of another project;[2] in the event this did not happen. However, much of the Welsh and northern British material, as well as many finds from Ireland and the near-Continent, were studied at first hand by the author in order to gain a finer appreciation of inter-comparisons and potential regional aspects of the assemblages. It was concluded that there were some important differences between the study assemblage and those in northern Britain and Ireland (e.g. Needham 2004, 219- 23), although many individual types can have close parallels in the three respective regions. The Welsh assemblage, however, presents little obvious differentiation from that in central and southern England and the scheme presented here may be readily applied to axes from all of southern Britain and probably beyond.

A detailed classification has been published for northern Britain (Schmidt & Burgess 1981), but this is not directly transferrable to the southern material for two main reasons. Firstly, the assemblage of axes in the south has a different composition in morphological terms even though many individual axe forms are the same in both regions; the text below will detail some of the differences. Secondly, however, Schmidt & Burgess's scheme seems not always to have been successful in grouping alike axes and distinguishing between unlike ones; the best parallels for a given southern type amongst the northern axes have frequently been found to include examples attributed to different types in that corpus. Lack of morphological coherence is even more acutely the case for the Irish classification produced by Harbison (1969). Given this pervading problem, it was felt crucial to put assessment of formal characteristics on an objective footing.

The author's methodology relied on two principal tenets. First and foremost the condition of an object must be evaluated before any attempt at classification is made; surface loss through corrosion, sometimes exacerbated through modern 'cleaning', can have a significant and variable effect on the original outline and can also obscure evidence for breaks which would be obvious on an object in good surface condition (not to be confused with a complete state). A layer of corrosion of constant thickness across the faces and sides of an axe will be doubled where two faces converge at any acutely tapered part of the object, notably the butt, cutting edge and flange crests; these then become particularly vulnerable to subsequent attrition (the principle is illustrated in Needham *et al.* 2015, Appendix S1, 2 fig S1). Shallow or subtle surface features will also be vulnerable to total loss – stop-bevels, edge bevels, decoration and original working and wear traces. This contrast can occasionally be seen strikingly on axes on which fragments of original oxidised surface (generally called 'patina') survive and

---

[1] Now available on-line through EThOS
[2] Bronze Age Metallurgy in Wales, Colin Burgess & Peter Northover

stand proud of *reduced* surfaces where that original surface has been removed by disintegration of any kind, such as flaking, crumbling or abrasion.

Despite these difficulties, an attempt must be made whenever possible at estimating original outlines in both plan and profile view. Providing it is done empirically and systematically, this procedure gives the best chance of finding the most useful classification criteria, which are often carefully chosen points within a spectrum. The same procedure must of course then be applied to any future finds if they are to be placed successfully within the classification scheme. Although reconstructed outlines may not be accurate (only where small bits are missing from an object in good surface condition), they will be *more* accurate than the extant outlines providing that reconstruction is informed by knowledge of axes in good condition. To give one example, Class 3 axes always taper to a fairly thin butt in profile unless reworked there after damage; consequently, it is reasonable to project the plane of the faces in profile beyond a butt fracture to obtain an estimate of its original length. Outline projection has, however, only been attempted when the missing part is small relative to the whole.

The second tenet is that if we seek to group objects that are similar in their external morphology (and this does not exclude other approaches to classification) then it is best to objectify the description of the relevant morphological attributes. As an example, if we are going to talk about *broad-butted* axes as distinct from *narrow-butted* ones, then it is essential to provide some kind of value for where the boundary between 'broad' and 'narrow' best lies. This kind of objectivity has been achieved by using a number of fairly simple metrical indices for shape and proportions. Evaluation of metrical ranges within a type and metrical boundaries between types is best undertaken using appropriate *dimension ratios* because absolute dimensions do not compensate for different sizes of object within a type. The critical dimension ratios are defined below.

While it may be assumed that early metal age people themselves would recognise many of the form differences being identified by us, it is not suggested that they would always recognise as significant the exact boundaries extracted from rigorous and objective classification methods. Metrical objectivity does, however, ensure that we are achieving what we aim to achieve, a formal classification that genuinely groups together similarly shaped objects and sets apart dissimilar ones. Using ratios as opposed to absolute dimensions certainly solves the problem of assessing morphological similarity or dissimilarity. However, it needs to be acknowledged that either human perception or functional requirements may sometimes lead to a drift in ratios seen against changing object size. For example, if it was crucial to keep the cutting edge at a certain width to serve particular functions, then that dimension may not have been reduced in proportion to length as the overall size of the axe was reduced. There is no perfect answer to this potential dilemma, but it needs to be kept in mind during data analysis and interpretation. The author's experience suggests that this kind of sliding relationship between a ratio and absolute size is not a significant feature of the early metal age axe sequence.

The use of statistical methods for finding the best grouping of the axes was rejected because it was felt that, firstly, not all the information contributing to it could be satisfactorily reduced to numerical indices, secondly, there are often problems in deciding whether to give different weighting to different kinds of attribute information, and thirdly, it gives little room for value judgements on where to place divisions based on broader archaeological information, for example association patterns or metal composition. There is the additional problem for a lengthy sequence of material spanning some centuries that one particular attribute may be incredibly important at one point of the sequence and wholly irrelevant at another. The more judgemental approach taken here allows different critical attributes to come into prominence and then wane in a rolling sequence.

The finest sub-divisions of types proposed in 1983 have been left out here. These divisions were referred to as 'styles' and were an attempt to group together, where relevant, axes of extremely similar proportions for which it was felt possible they would be products of the same group of metalworkers and even occasionally derived from the same mould or pattern. There are, however, problems with such a premise, especially when a production tradition results in a high degree of standardisation around one or few ideal models. In such cases some objects are bound to come out very similar to one another simply because their producers were successful in adhering tightly to the ideal model(s); the resulting similarity need imply no more than that two objects were products of that coherent tradition.

Ultimately, any level of classification only becomes meaningful through correlations with other independent data – for the material under consideration here the key data are context, time period, metal composition, geography and decoration.

Decoration, embellishment or careful finishing beyond the needs of practical use are the norm on early metal age axes and can be considered integral to their character throughout the series. There are two modes of execution for decoration or embellishment: tracer-punching to form patterns of short linear strokes or occasionally dots, and hammer-forging to form larger faceted or fluted areas. Decoration/embellishment can occur on either the faces or the sides, and is often present on both. Taking only axes in reasonable surface condition, the proportion of axes lacking any kind of embellishment is surprisingly low: even at the beginning, in the Moel Arthur Assemblage, it is only around 50%; it then decreases to 33% in the Brithdir Assemblage, to below 20% in the Mile Cross Assemblage, and to just a few percent in the Willerby Assemblage. This zenith in decorating and embellishing axes may continue into the beginning of the Arreton Assemblage, but then there was a small reversal so that overall about 15% of Arreton Assemblage axes are totally without. The full sequence of changing styles of ornamentation is rich and complex (Megaw & Hardy 1938; Needham 1983, chapter 14) and only a brief summary will be given here.

The earliest embellishments occur on Class 2 copper axes – simple but neat facets and furrows (see Type series nos. 7-14). For half of Class 3 axe currency embellishment remains equally simple although triple longitudinal faceting of the sides is added to double (nos. 26 & 34). However, late in the Brithdir Assemblage, more formal punched decoration emerges on Class 3 axes (notably 3E), initially as 'rain-pattern' designs (Needham 1987). This is quickly diversified into other designs such as herringbone or chevron rows during the Mile Cross Assemblage. New arrangements of fluting, notably longitudinally splayed designs, are also occasionally found. At this stage decoration occurs on both Class 3 (notably 3F) and Class 4 (i.e. 4B) axes. A little later side decoration becomes more ornate with the creation of strings of lozenge facets; when the axe is viewed in plan, these lozenge strings give the sides a gently scalloped outline (e.g. Type series nos 60, 61, 63 & 65).

By the Willerby Assemblage, face decoration is frequently set within a more formalised panel, sometimes with a complex infill of punched strokes. In many cases this panel is restricted to the upper part of the blade and is bordered on the underside (hence above the edge bevel) by a broad and shallow horizontal hammered furrow. Although subtle, this feature contrasts with and complements the panel in the way light plays on it. Diagonal fluting ('cabling') of sides is occasionally found on low-flanged axes but becomes more frequent as flanges become higher and sides correspondingly broader on Class 5 axes

(Arreton Assemblage). There is a late resurgence in more complex patterns of shallow hammered furrows on faces on Class 5 axes. They are frequently used in multiple to create fluted panels, the furrows sometimes aligned diagonally as well as orthogonally. Occasionally the two modes of execution are used in combination, furrows serving as an underlay to punched designs.

Notes on the illustrative type series

The main purpose of the axe drawings in Figures 17 – 32 is to illustrate as clearly as possible the defining characteristics of the types identified in this classification scheme. For this reason the axes illustrated, although based on actual examples (Appendix 1), have been 'made good' if there were any minor irregularities caused by fracture, burring or corrosion loss; wherever possible the axes chosen were in good to very good surface condition and complete or very nearly so. Similarly, some incidental features, notably slight twists down the length of the body, may have been suppressed in some drawings. To some extent, therefore, the axes shown are ideal examples. A second point is that the drawings are deliberately not to a consistent scale. Since the classification scheme depends entirely on proportions rather than absolute dimensions, inter-comparison is greatly facilitated by showing the different shapes at approximately the same size. Nevertheless, a few axes are deliberately shown larger or smaller than the majority to make the point that exceptional sizes are an important part of the range for the type in question. Not all variation within a defined sub-class or type is shown, but the full ranges are covered by the metrical attributes provided in Table 1.

Table 1: Flat and low-flanged axes from southern Britain: critical relative dimensions.
NB The values given reflect the core distributions for the type; occasional axes may have values falling just outside for one attribute

Class	Relative butt width		Cutting edge proportions		Body proportions		Side curvature	
	RWB	RWB′	RWE	RDE	EH	RW3	RMO	ASD
1A	≥ 0.38	≥ 0.21	0.55 – 0.70	≥ 0.30	≤ 0.10	n/r	0.07 – 0.10	≥ 0.65
2A	≥ 0.46	≥ 0.27	0.55 – 0.70	≥ 0.30	≤ 0.10	n/r	0.05 – 0.10	n/c
2B	≥ 0.46	≥ 0.27	0.55 – 0.70	≤ 0.30	≥ 0.09	n/r	> 0.025	n/c
2C	≥ 0.46	≥ 0.27	0.55 – 0.70	≤ 0.31	≥ 0.11	n/r	> 0.025	n/c
2D	≥ 0.46	≥ 0.27	0.55 – 0.70	≤ 0.32	≥ 0.14	n/r	< 0.025	n/c
2E	n/r	n/r	> 0.70	n/r	n/r	n/r	n/r	n/r
3A	0.38 – 0.46	0.21 – 0.29	0.50 – 0.65	≤ 0.30	< 0.16	0.51 – 0.61	0.04 – 0.08	≤ 0.65
3B	< 0.38	≤ 0.29	≥ 0.66	≤ 0.22	variable	0.58 – 0.75	> 0.06	≤ 0.65
3C	≤ 0.35	≤ 0.23	0.58 – 0.65	≤ 0.22	> 0.15	0.52 – 0.62	< 0.06	≤ 0.65
3D	≤ 0.35	≤ 0.23	0.52 – 0.65	≤ 0.22	0.12 – 0.15	0.50 – 0.58	< 0.06	≤ 0.65
3E	< 0.38	≤ 0.23	0.52 – 0.65	≤ 0.22	< 0.12	0.46 – 0.55	0.05 – 0.10	≤ 0.65
3F	≤ 0.34	≤ 0.19	0.52 – 0.60	≤ 0.16	< 0.12	≤ 0.47	0.05 – 0.10	≤ 0.65
3G	0.34 – 0.42	≤ 0.21	≤ 0.55	0.20 – 0.25	≤ 0.10	≤ 0.45	0.04 – 0.07	≤ 0.65
4A	n/r	n/r	≥ 0.60	0.16 – 0.30	n/r	≥ 0.48	0.07 – 0.10	≤ 0.65
4B	n/r	n/r	0.50 – 0.60	≤ 0.22	n/r	0.41 – 0.48	0.04 – 0.10	≤ 0.65
4C	n/r	n/r	≤ 0.55	0.13 – 0.25	n/r	0.34 – 0.41	0.04 – 0.10	0.45 – 0.75
4D	n/r	n/r	≤ 0.51	0.20 – 0.34	n/r	0.34 – 0.42	0.02 – 0.06	≥ 0.65
4E	n/r	n/r	≥ 0.50	0.17 – 0.37	n/r	0.33 – 0.44	0.06 – 0.15	≥ 0.65
4F	n/r	n/r	0.48 – 0.58	0.26 – 0.34	n/r	≤ 0.32	≥ 0.06	≥ 0.65
axe-chisels	n/r	n/r	≤ 0.45	n/r	n/r	n/r	n/r	n/r

n/r – not relevant to this sub-classification
n/c – not calculated due to large uncertainty in RMO position or too small a sample size

Terminology for features and critical metrical attributes

To avoid ambiguity, terminology for the different parts of an object must always be carefully defined and consistently applied. This is most easily done diagrammatically (Fig 1). For early axes, it is important to differentiate between the *haft end* and the *butt*, and between the *blade* and the *blade edge*. The haft-end and blade together create the *body*. Another area of confusion caused by variable terminology concerns the description of the line taken by the body's sides. Terms such as 'expanding', 'flared', 'out-swinging' or 'splayed' are frequently used interchangeably to describe the overall shape of the axe's body. However, early metal age axes universally increase in width from butt to cutting edge, so there is always expansion to some degree; in fact, there are two largely separable elements that need to be adequately defined and described. The first is the degree of *divergence of the body*, either of the whole body or a specified part (such as the haft-end); the second is the *shape of the sides*– whether concave, straight, angled, convex, sinuous etc. Figure 2 illustrates how these two largely independent variables may be combined to create a range of (theoretical) body shapes. In the British series considered here, sides are normally concave to some degree, but the strength and shape of curvature varies.

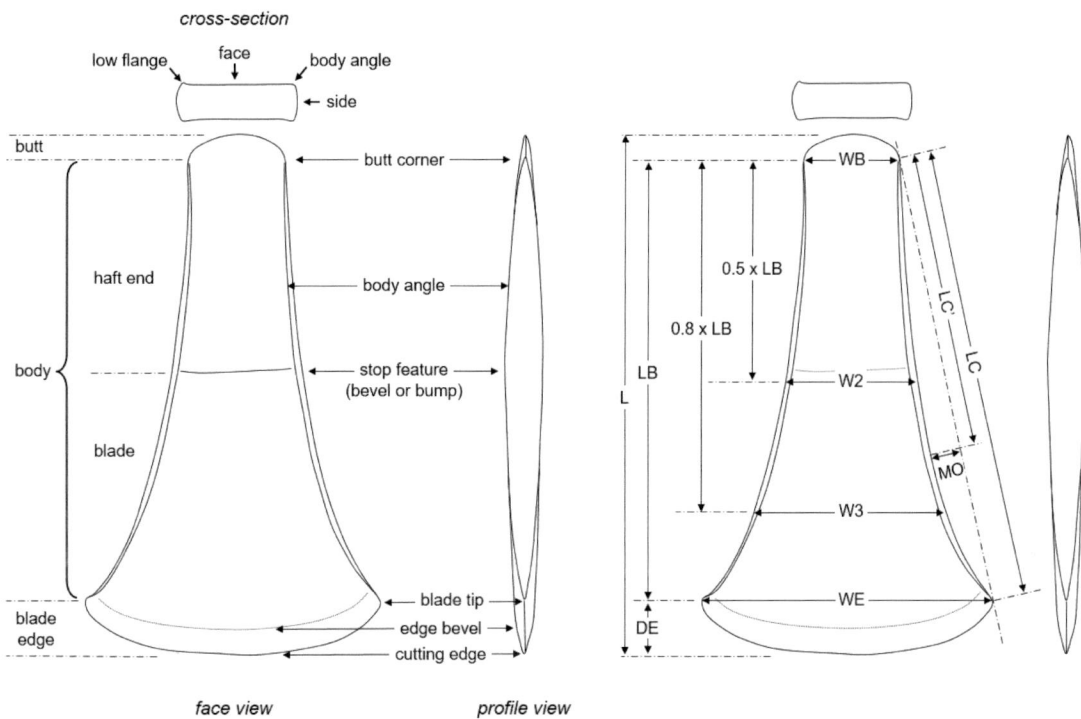

Figure 1: Definition of the parts and dimensions of Chalcolithic and Early Bronze Age axes

A further complication in defining side shapes concerns the *blade tips*. Any hammer-working of the cutting edge during post-cast working will inevitably lead not only to thinning of the edge, but also to expansion of the tips. There is frequently a distinct out-turn at the very bottom of the blade coinciding closely with the edge bevel. Since it cannot usually be known whether this was an originally intended feature (a design feature) or one that emerged incidentally and progressively through use and re-sharpening, it is prudent to exclude the blade tips from any basic description of an axe's body shape. For this reason, one chronologically sensitive metrical attribute, that of *relative blade width*, uses a point on the blade somewhat above the tips (see below for definition – RW3). The definitions for side curvature employed, however, include the blade tips simply because in many cases there is no clearly defined break from the line of the blade sides. It therefore needs to be kept in mind

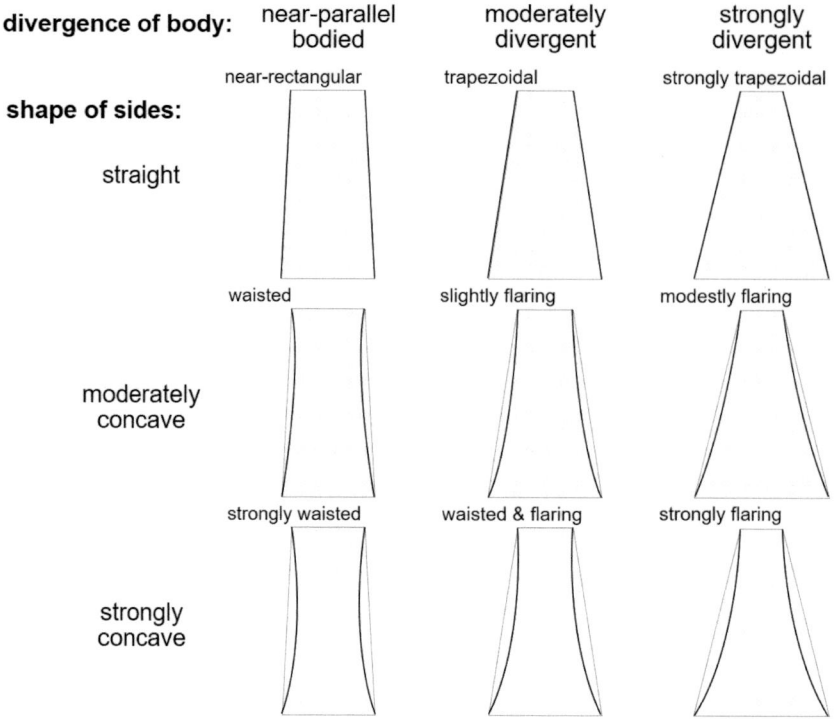

Figure 2: Hypothetical variations in axe body forms in relation to divergence of the body and shape of the sides; the descriptions in the boxes are not intended to be defined terms

that variations in side curvature (as expressed by RMO and ASD below) may involve a combination of intended form and, to a small extent, unavoidable modifications during the use-life.

Definitions of critical dimension ratios
Most ratios used for this morphological classification are defined in relation to a length measurement, either total length (L), length of body (LB) or length of the chord across the sides (LC) (Fig 1). Two ratios are defined instead in relation to width of cutting edge (WE), and one is in relation to width in the middle of the body (W2). In the original study, other variables were investigated through further ratios, but since these have no impact on the classification as such, they are not covered here. They can, however, further qualify the particular properties of a given type of axe.

Width of butt relative to width of cutting edge (**RWB** = WB/WE). In cases where the sides curve into the butt to give rather rounded corners, a judgement has to be made on the point of transition.

Width of butt relative to length (**RWB′** = WB/L). This is a valuable second measure of butt width which circumvents axes being categorised as broad-butted or narrow-butted simply because they have unusually narrow or wide cutting edges respectively; in practice it is the combination of RWB and RWB′ values that best defines butt width overall.

Relative width of cutting edge (**RWE** = WE/L). This ratio has great utility at a broad level, but may be less useful at a refined level because it includes any minor contribution from the post-cast and use-life expansion of the blade tips.

Relative depth of cutting edge (**RDE** = DE/WE). This is the simplest way of describing the *average* degree of curvature of the cutting edge; it does not, however, deal with changes in curvature along the edge – for example, some edges are slight in curvature in their central stretches and become tighter curves towards either tip. Depth is measured to a line drawn across the blade tips, being the most angular or tightly curving points between the cutting edge and the sides.

Expansion of haft end (**EH** = (W2-WB)/LB). To ensure consistency between axes with and without stop bevels, the 'haft end' for this measure is taken to be half the length of the body; measurement W2 is therefore positioned exactly halfway along the defined length LB.

Relative width of mid-blade (**RW3** = W3/LB). Since relative width appears to be an important indicator of temporal trends, it was felt advisable to position the measurement, W3, as far down the blade as possible but avoiding any possible influence from blade tip expansion; W3 is therefore positioned 80% of the distance along LB from the butt.

Relative maximum offset (**RMO** = MO/LC). LC (length of chord) is the length of the line drawn from the butt corner to the blade tip. The RMO ratio proves to be a good guide to overall side curvature, but any damage to these apices can introduce significant uncertainty in the estimation of the original maximum offset, MO. Wherever possible, the RMO value should be obtained on both sides and the average taken.

Asymmetry of side curvature (**ASC** = LC´/LC). Having established the position at which the maximum offset occurs, LC´ is its distance along LC from the butt end; thus high values (e.g. 0.8) show strong asymmetry relative to values closer to 0.5, which indicate more evenly curved (or angled) sides. Although this value cannot be very precisely calculated due to difficulty in judging exactly where the offset is at its maximum, again it is a good broad indicator of a crucial variation in side shape. Wherever possible both sides should be measured and the average taken.

Mean relative width of body (**MRW** = (WB+W2+W3)/LB). By taking an average of three width measurements down the length of the body, a good index of overall relative body width is obtained. This value will not, however, pick up differences between bodies that are expanding significantly and those that are more parallel-sided (see Fig 2); this question requires another calculated variable, *expansion of body (EB)*, which is not used here.

Rectangularity of body section (**RBS** = MT/W2). This ratio gives the maximum thickness of the axe's body relative to its width at the middle. MT is the maximum thickness along the median line of the body. W2 is used in preference to WS so that all axes can be compared systematically, both those with and without stops. W2 is often not at the point of maximum thickness, so this ratio does not necessarily reflect a single cross-section through the body.

Relative height of flanges (**RHF** = HF/LB). HF is the maximum height of any of the four flanges above the septum, so RHF is similarly a maximum value. It is scaled in relation to body length (LB), since flanges on Early Bronze Age axes flank most of the body.

Basic descriptive categories of axe
The axes covered in the present work are *flat, low-flanged* or *long-flanged*. In the past some researchers have used the term 'hammer-flanged' to cover axes here called 'low-flanged'. However, as Butler argued (1963, 28), 'hammer-flanged' presupposes metallurgical information on the mode of formation of the flanges. Since it is hypothetically possible that

even low flanges might be cast in the mould, it is preferable to stick to the more neutral term adopted by Butler – *low-flanged*.

The distinction between *flat* and *low-flanged* axes is only certain for axes in excellent to good condition. Low flanges as originally formed can be as little as 0.5mm high, or even less. As noted above, slight features along the edges of a bronze object will inevitably be particularly susceptible to loss through corrosion reduction or abrasion; there are clear cases of axes with poor surface condition having lost their low flanges wholly or in part. For this reason, the flat/low-flanged distinction should be regarded merely as a convenient descriptor and not as a universally reliable classification for chronological or other analytical purposes.

An interpretative issue with regard to low flanging is that of intentionality; post-cast working of the sides might result in slight lipping of the body angles without any deliberate intention to create such features. This is suspected on a small number of well-preserved axes. In fact, such *incipient* flanging, if unwanted, could easily have been removed by the metalworker by grinding or hammering. So, if low flanges are consistently present along much of the sides of an axe this suggests they were either intended from the outset or regarded as an acceptable feature arising from post-cast working.

In summary, 'flat' and 'low-flanged' are useful *basic descriptive terms*; they reflect development only at the broad trajectory level and are not critical to classification at either the class or sub-class levels, this being based on a variety of other feature combinations. Surface deterioration may preclude knowing whether an axe had low flanges, yet may not be so severe as to prevent grouping on the basis of outline shape. It is noteworthy that during one phase (Mile Cross Metalwork Assemblage) the three main shapes of axe (Sub-classes 3F, 3G and 4B) are a genuine mix of axes with and without low-flanges.

The distinction between low-flanged and long-flanged axes is generally much more easily determined and RHF is used as the defining feature between Classes 3-4 and Class 5 axes (see below). The term *long-flanged* serves to distinguish them from most flanged axe types of the Middle Bronze Age on which the flanges have been shortened so that they mainly just flank the haft-end. These were called *haft-flanged* and *wing-flanged* by Smith (1959), but the collective term *short-flanged* has since proved useful (Schmidt & Burgess 1981, 75). Where axes are merely referred to as 'flanged' in this paper, it implies long-flanged.

Principal classes of axe
The classification scheme constructed in 1983 is hierarchical and begins by defining five *principal classes* of axe. This has the combined virtues of, firstly, allowing examples in poor condition to be classified to this level if not beyond and, secondly, allowing axe evolution to be considered in terms of its broad trajectory. The defining features – a combination of overall shape (especially butt width) and key 'technological' features (long profile, stop and flanges) – are summarised in Table 2 and only a little amplification is needed.

These principal classes essentially define the mode and security of the hafting of the axe-head. In broad terms the classes form a temporal succession, but evidence from associations suggests that Classes 1 and 2 were substantially concurrent, while Classes 3 and 4 had significantly overlapping currencies (Fig 3). This illustrates that although there was a progressive improvement in hafting method, this was by no means the sole driving force in the stylistic development of early metal age axes.

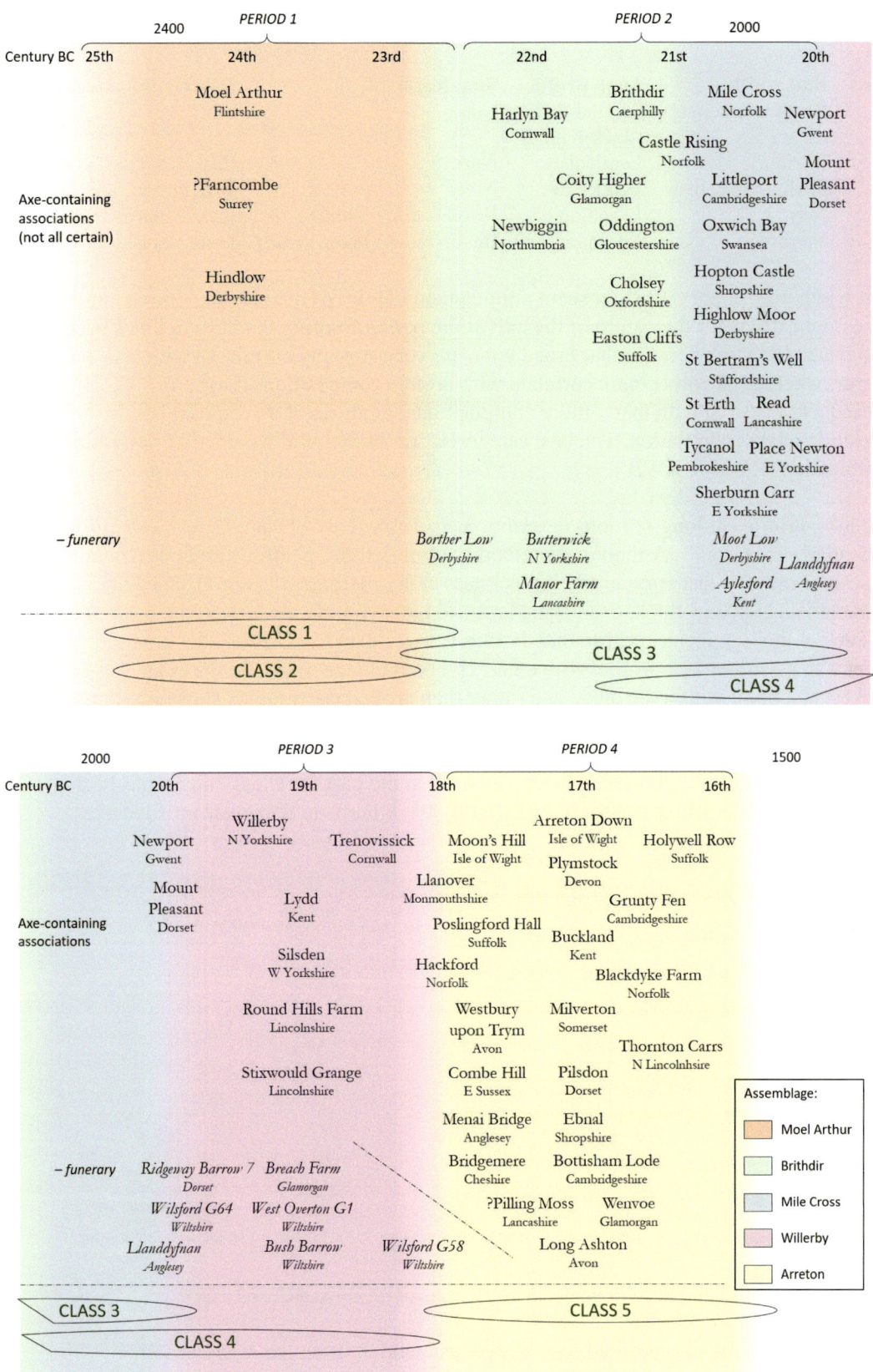

Figure 3: The chronology of the principal classes of Chalcolithic and Early Bronze Age axe and their associated finds in England and Wales; note that all certain and potential associations are shown

Table 2: Defining features of the principal classes of early metal age axe

Class	Butt width	Long profile	Stop feature	Descriptive category
1	Broad to medium	Parallel-faced (thick-butted)	None	Flat
2	Broad	Lenticular	None	Flat
3	Medium to narrow	Lenticular	None	Flat, or low-flanged
4	Narrow	Lozengic	Bevel (rarely: bump)	Low-flanged, or flat
5	Narrow	Lozengic	Bevel (rarely: bump or rib)	Long-flanged

Butt width may not at first sight seem a fundamental point of distinction, although it does have implications for the nature of the haft at the point of union. In addition it has been recognised for some decades that broad butts are very strongly correlated with axes of copper, whereas narrower butts correlate with bronze compositions (Britton 1963, 260-1). Subsequent research with many more compositional analyses at its disposal has further consolidated this correlation. The best categorisation of butt widths relies on two ratios in combination (RWB & RWB').

The long-profile (or long-section) descriptions in Table 2 are to some extent simplifications, particularly for Class 1. Although described as 'parallel-faced', this is an approximation since these axes often in fact vary a little in thickness along their length (Fig 4). The butt is characteristically very thick, even if the haft end tapers a little towards it; a key point is the absence of the 'lenticular' profile that defines Classes 2 and 3. Class 1 axes sometimes display an asymmetrical profile, with convexity on one face only, and they can also be thickest at a point within the blade end rather than around the middle. Those which present a steady and symmetrical taper towards the butt can get close to the profiles of certain Class 2 axes that still have slightly thickened butts (Fig 4) and it is possible there is a gradation in this respect. The term 'thick-butted', sometimes used in the past for Class 1 axes, has been avoided due to this minor occurrence of slightly thick butts on lenticular profiled axes.

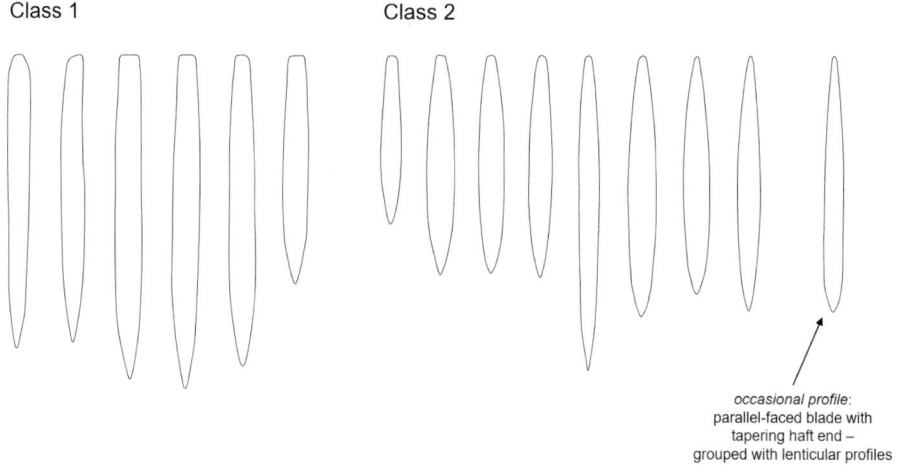

Figure 4: Examples of long profiles of Class 1 and Class 2 axes

Turning to the lenticular profiled forms, Classes 2 and 3, these are rarely absolutely symmetrical end to end because of the need for thicker metal behind the cutting edge for strength. Nevertheless, the maximum thickness is normally close to the middle (the centre of gravity is of course not near the middle because the blade is always broader than the haft-end). The same is true of lozenge profiled axes, Class 4; they are rarely strictly rhombic, but there is always a slight angle or inflection in profile at the stop feature. In well preserved examples the latter is almost always a defined bevel (*stop-bevel*), but it can occasionally be a rounded angle or alternatively a slightly raised ridge or bump (*stop-bump*).[3]

Although Class 3 and 4 axes can be either flat or low-flanged, as noted above, there is a temporal trend in this respect. Class 3 axes of the Brithdir Assemblage (Sub-classes 3A – 3E) are virtually all flat and only occasional late examples (within Sub-class 3E) are low-flanged. In the succeeding Mile Cross Assemblage, Sub-class 3F and 3G axes are probably more often low-flanged than not. Likewise, Sub-class 4B axes of that Assemblage are a mix of flat and low-flanged. By the Willerby Assemblage the great majority of axes (Sub-classes 4C – 4F) are low-flanged.

In contrast to all preceding low-flanged axes, Class 5 axes have moderate to well-developed flanges which were patently an intended feature and were probably for the most part present in the casting.[4] The distribution of relative flange heights for Classes 3, 4 and 5 axes is bimodal with a trough between RHF 0.01 and 0.02 (Fig 5). Class 5 axes are therefore defined as having RHF > 0.015, a ratio which, on a fairly typical axe of body length 100mm, equates to a maximum flange height of 1.5mm. Axes clearly reduced by surface stripping whose surviving flanges are less high may be accepted as Class 5 if all other shape characteristics fit better than with Class 4.

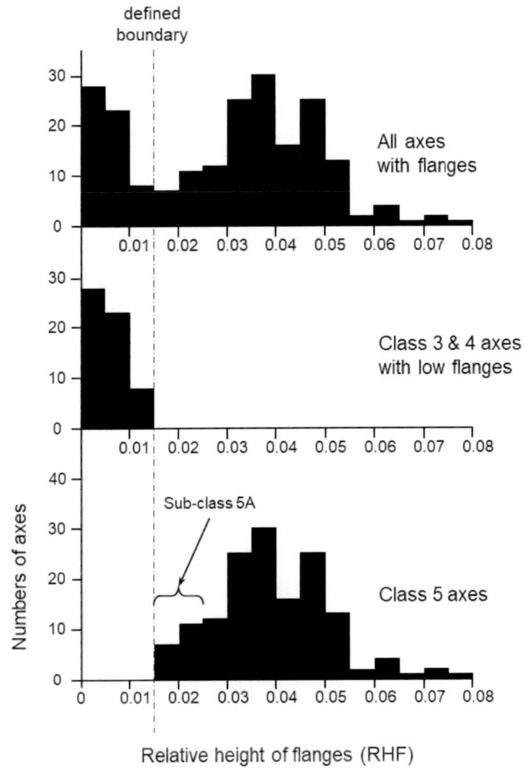

Figure 5: Distribution of RHF values (relative height of flanges) for all low-flanged and flanged axes in the 1983 corpus in fair to excellent condition (based on Needham 1983, fig 142a)

Sub-classes and types

Within any axe class attribution to *sub-class* depends on the detailed shape of the object in plan view. As already explained, shapes have been defined using critical relative dimensions and these are summarised in Table 1. Usually this has resulted in the definition of relatively homogeneous sets of axes which it is appropriate also to give a *Type* label, named after a classic find; in these cases the 'type' is synonymous with the sub-class, and may be more memorable.

Sometimes, however, the shapes thus defined still vary in one or more attributes of potential significance (for example, straighter sides versus concave sides) and, in such cases, that variation may be covered by naming more than one type within the sub-class (as seen within Sub-classes 2C, 3A, 4E, 5B and 5D). A further situation occurs where an individual axe fits the metrical criteria for a sub-class, but does not look particularly similar to others thus

---

[3] The term 'stop-ridge' is largely avoided here because it is used widely for later flanged axes and palstaves with much higher stop features than present in the series under consideration

[4] No moulds are known; post-cast working would probably have frequently modified the height and shape of flanges

grouped; these can be left *untyped* within that sub-class. Finally, Sub-class 2E is particularly poorly represented and yet still inhomogeneous in terms of outline shape; it has therefore been left *without* any type designation as yet. This can be remedied if any more consistent shapes become apparent within the sub-class as the dataset increases.

In summary, therefore, the sub-class designation rests primarily on metrical evaluation, while the type designation defines groups that are stylistically very similar and these may or may not be the same thing. By allowing the possibility of more than one type per sub-class, further specific 'types' can be added in future as they are recognised without necessarily reconfiguring the sub-class structure. For example, detailed study of the Irish Killaha type axes may well reveal significant variations in shape (see comments in Sub-class 3B below), and this may in turn have repercussions on the smaller number of parallel axes from Britain.

The classification

Axes of both Classes 1 and 2 are defined on the basis of having relatively broad butts. They are also, almost universally, made of copper rather than bronze. Although broad butts are characteristic, the two classes do not share exactly the same range of butt widths; Class 1 axes can have butts which extend down into the *medium-broad* range as defined here, whereas Class 2 are entirely within the *broad* range.

Class 1 axes

Rather few axes from southern Britain have the diagnostic 'parallel' faces and thick butts that define Class 1; just ten were catalogued in the original corpus and most of these are of uncertain provenance (Needham 1983). They are no more frequent elsewhere in Britain. Despite their rarity and the likelihood they were imports rather than early indigenous products, it was felt useful nevertheless to define a class because of the type's importance for the earliest metallurgy of these islands. Only one sub-class is defined as yet, but different forms in Ireland and the near-Continent, and a possible Scottish find (Schmidt & Burgess 1981, no 6), allow the theoretical possibility of the future discovery of other Class 1 sub-classes in southern Britain.

Sub-class 1A, Type Minto (Type series nos. 1-3)
The fairly broad butt is sub-square or only slightly arched; the body is at first parallel sided or only marginally expanding, but then flares out, often strongly, to the blade tips; the cutting edge is characteristically deeply curved. These are generally relatively large objects, rather clumsy in appearance and often not well finished, although this is not invariable. Usually there is no attempt to define a clear edge bevel, the profile towards the cutting edge instead being a continuous curve. The variation encountered in long profiles (looking also at the more numerous external parallels; Fig 4) has been described above, where the point was also made that the neater profiles may grade into those of Class 2. Indeed, amongst the more prolific Irish series there are axes deviating only a little from the above definition that include more refined finishing including edge bevels (e.g. Fig 6d). This question of gradation requires thorough analysis of the Irish corpus and cannot be pursued further here.

Since Schmidt & Burgess's definition for their *Type Minto* is closely equivalent to that given above, that type-name has been retained here for such finds throughout Britain. More numerous Irish parallels can be found amongst Harbison's Type Lough Ravel (Harbison 1969), but that label is best replaced because his defined group is very eclectic. The present writer proposes the term *Type Cappeen* for a much more tightly defined Irish group using the criteria set out above (Fig 6).

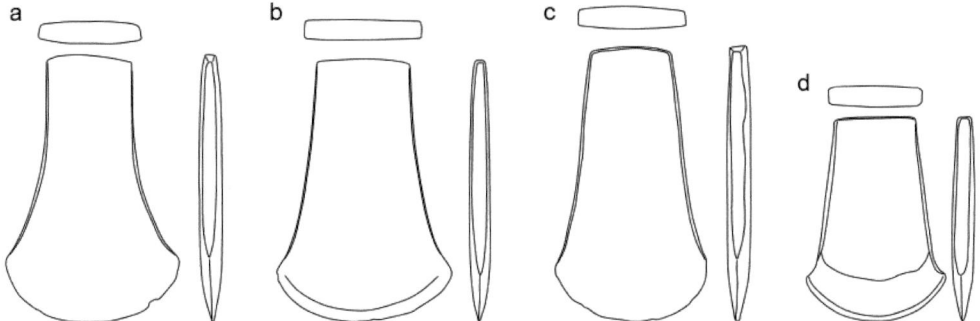

Figure 6: Examples of Irish Type Cappeen axes and variants thereof: a) classic form, Cappeen hoard, Co Cork; b) shallower cutting edge, Clashbredane hoard, Co Cork; c) more flared body, Castletown Roche hoard, Co Cork; d) refined shaping, Co Armagh. Scale 25%. Drawings Stuart Needham, (a) & (b) based on O'Brien 2004, (c) based on Case 1966

The only secure association in Britain for Sub-class 1A Type Minto remains the Moel Arthur hoard, Denbighshire (Forde-Johnston 1962), where two examples are associated with an axe of Sub-class 2A (type series nos. 1 & 5). Two of the three axes are a little atypical in not having particularly deep cutting edges (RDE *c*. 0.30), but this is also the case for some Irish examples very like Type Cappeen (Fig 6b).

Class 2 axes
By far the dominant form of copper axe across Britain is that having a neatly produced lenticular long profile. Haft-end profiles can terminate in either a thin rounded butt or a slightly thicker and flatter-topped butt (Fig 4), a distinction that has no obvious correlation with other variables. Occasionally the two faces are not equally curved, asymmetry likely being residual from the blank having been cast in a univalve mould. End-to-end longitudinal asymmetry can also occur: while normally thickest around the middle of the axe, a minority of axes are thickest within the blade half. There is also a small sub-set in which the profile is parallel-faced at the blade end flowing smoothly into a tapered haft end (Fig 4, far right); being rare, these axes have not been thought to justify a separate profile categorisation.

Edge bevels are often neatly delineated and there can be additional faceted embellishments above that bevel, outlining the butt, or along the sides. Class 2 axes are distinguished from Class 3 by their broader butts – RWB greater than 0.46 *and* RWB' greater than 0.27. In the rare instances where only one of these criteria is satisfied, attribution to Class 2 or 3 needs be on the basis of overall best fit.

Given their numbers, Class 2 axes can be regarded as the standard axe form current in the British Chalcolithic (Period 1). The temptation to see these generally more refined products as a temporal development from Class 1 axes should be resisted. A few hoards and possible associations, mainly in Ireland but including Moel Arthur, include both classes (nos. 1 & 5; Needham 1996, 126 table 1) and there is a further issue concerning the form of the immediate Continental progenitors to insular axes. Most finds of copper axes from the nearer parts of the Continent are difficult to date closely, but it would appear that by the time metallurgy was introduced to Britain and Ireland, lenticular-profiled axes were already frequent in many parts of Western Europe. Indeed, it is possible that they were the absolute norm in some regions; for example, few thick-butted axes can be identified in northern or western France. On this basis, it may be that the default form introduced to Britain was Class 2, rather than Class 1. If anything it is the distinctive form of Irish parallel-faced axes, including Type Cappeen, that requires special explanation and this will be addressed elsewhere.

Class 2 axes have been divided into five sub-classes according to shape in plan. 2A and 2B are the most similar in shape to Sub-class 1A axes, while 2C and 2D have more trapezoidal bodies often in combination with more arched butts. Sub-class 2E axes are unusually squat. The distinctions are for the most part not clear-cut and they represent trends within Class 2 rather than necessarily discrete morphological populations.

Sub-class 2A, Type Burley Camp (Type series nos. 4-6)
A few Class 2 axes have a very similar shape to that of Sub-class 1A, notably with near-parallel haft ends, flaring blades and a deeply curved cutting edge. They also show asymmetrical features of the kind frequently found on their Class 1 counterparts. Bodies are relatively thick, the maximum thickness being closer to the cutting edge than the butt. One of the three axes in the Moel Arthur hoard, Denbighshire, associated with two 1A axes, is best placed in this sub-class even though the depth of the cutting edge is borderline (RDE 0.30). The type-name is after a find from Burley Camp, Devon (no 4; Plymouth Museum).

Examples matching this definition seem to be equally rare in northern Britain, where they are amongst Schmidt & Burgess's Type Ballybeg/Roseisle (1981, especially nos. 23 & 24), and while there seem to be rather more amongst the Irish corpus (e.g. Harbison 1969, nos. 47, 85, 226, 247, 306, 390), it is difficult to evaluate how frequent they are there. An important association from Knocknagur, Co Galway, contains two axes of Sub-class 2A along with a tanged dagger, a diminutive axe and three awls (Coffey 1901, pl XXXII, 44 & 45). The dagger is a developed example datable to later rather than earlier in the Chalcolithic (Needham *et al*. 2017, 23). Harbison's subtype name 'Ballybeg' is inappropriate here for two reasons; he uses it for axe shapes covering the full Class 2 spectrum defined in this paper and, moreover, the surviving axe from the Ballybeg hoard itself has a medium-broad butt and would be classified here as Sub-class 3A.

Sub-class 2B, Type Lode (Type series nos. 7-9)
Several axes have a similar shape to Sub-classes 1A and 2A but are worth separating on account of some subtle distinctions. Most notably, the cutting edge is shallower (RDE < 0.30) and while this could be a trend associated with more re-sharpening over an extended use-life, the presence of other distinguishing features suggests this is not the full explanation. Butt lines are relatively straight and neat, and bodies expand gradually, the sides only slightly concave except where they turn out for the blade tips. This out-turn was presumably caused during preparation of the cutting edge. Occasional axes have blade tips only minimally out-turned and these can be difficult to place between Sub-classes 2B and 2D. At least three of the axes from England, including the type find from Bottisham Lode, Lode parish, Cambridgeshire (no 7; Fox 1923, 53, pl VI.1) have a second bevel above the edge bevel, thereby defining a very shallow furrow echoing the line of the edge; such features are neatly executed and judged to be deliberate embellishments.

Very similar axes can be identified in Ireland (e.g. Harbison 1969, nos. 222, 246, 245, 300, 388, 398, 411) and there are others with comparable body form but with deeper cutting edges. It is noteworthy that the three most similar axes from northern Britain also have this deeper cutting edge (Schmidt & Burgess 1981, nos. 4, 13, 21) and should not therefore be attributed to Type Lode. The possibility that the southern British finds have suffered more use and reworking, thus resulting in the reduction of the central stretch of the edge, is not an entirely satisfactory explanation given neat fashioning of the furrows above some cutting edges.

Another possibility is that regionally based metalworking groups working within parallel traditions tended to produce differently proportioned cutting edges. This need not have been a conscious act.

No contemporary contexts are known in Britain, an example from Hayne, Somerset, having been redeposited in the Late Bronze Age. At least one axe in the Tallaght, Co Dublin, hoard and one of the surviving Clashbredane hoard axes, Co Cork (Harbison 1969, nos. 146 & 44), are of the variant with the deeper cutting edge. Other axes in Irish hoards have similar shapes in plan, but in combination with Class 1 profiles.

Sub-class 2C, Types Purdis Farm and Ironbridge (Type series nos. 10-14)
Sub-class 2C axes are only subtly different from 2B and 2D. Although the body is near trapezoidal, sides are in fact gently curved (RMO > 0.025); in some cases the RMO value has been enhanced by blade tip expansion, but removing this element does not affect the fine separation of Sub-class 2C from 2D (Needham 1983, 101, fig 154). Morphologically the two sub-classes may form a continuous spectrum, but there are some qualitative differences that encourage separate definition. Surface deterioration can exacerbate the difficulty of attribution, since the modest out-turned blade tips and slight butt expansion of 2C axes can easily be reduced, thus leading to a resemblance to 2D axes.

Most 2C butt widths (RWB) fall within the range 0.48 – 0.56, but a few are greater than 0.59 giving the axe an overall broader look; these ranges are used to define *Types Purdis Farm* (type find from Suffolk – Ipswich Museum; type series no 10) and *Ironbridge* (type find from Shropshire – Shrewsbury Museum; no 13) respectively. Butts are modestly arched and frequently associated with very slight expansion of the butt corners; this presumably derives from final working of the faces alongside the butt, but if merely an incidental feature, there is nevertheless finesse in the shaping. Cutting edges are relatively shallow: RDE less than 0.30 and usually less than 0.25. Blade tips are usually out-turned, sometimes strongly so. Butts are sometimes neatly flat-topped, but this does not affect the overall lenticular profile. A good proportion of 2C axes in southern Britain (and elsewhere) have the furrow embellishment above the edge bevel, noted already amongst Sub-class 2B, and a few have neat double-faceting of the sides.

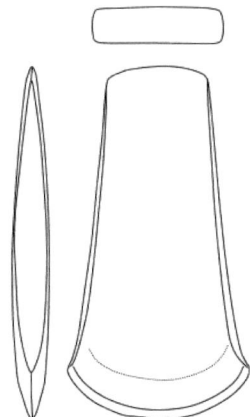

Figure 7: Axe from Mombach, Kr. Mainz, Germany; scale 50%; drawing Stuart Needham

A few axes in northern Britain are similar to Type Purdis Farm (e.g. Schmidt & Burgess 1981, nos. 43, 44, 48, 49, 50 & 53). These are the examples with broadest butts amongst their Type Dunnottar, the three analysed examples of which are of bronze, rather than copper. This composition is consistent with the remainder of Type Dunnottar, characterised by slightly narrower butts (RWB ≤ 0.46), but contrasts with Type Purdis Farm, whose axes are still of copper. A second difference is that, as seen for Sub-class 2B parallels in the north, the broad-butted Type Dunnottar axes again tend to have deeper cutting edges. A number of Irish parallels for Type Purdis Farm do, however, have the shallow cutting edge (Harbison 1969, nos. 360, 361, 371, 379, 403, 407, 430, 439) and this might provide the stronger link in terms of schools of production.

Attention may be drawn to two axes from the Continent which are closely related to Sub-class 2C, if not actually insular exports. They come from Mombach, Kr. Mainz, Germany (Fig 7), and further afield at Budkovice, Moravia, Czech Republic (Kibbert 1980, no 42;

Ondracek 1961, 151, Obr. 3; Muller-Karpe 1974, Tf 514C). The former has a metal composition matching the Irish Ross Island signature ('A-metal'); the latter is established to be of copper and was associated with a *Scheibenknopfnadel*. Again the suggestion is that this may be an export from Britain or Ireland (Case 1970, 661; Schmidt & Burgess 1981, 32), although the compositional difference noted above now militates against an origin in northern Britain.

An insular association for Type Purdis Farm occurs in the Carrickshedoge hoard, Co Wexford (Harbison 1969, no 360; personal study).

The best candidate for Sub-class 2C Type Ironbridge in northern Britain is provenanced only to 'Aberdeenshire' (Schmidt & Burgess 1981, no 9). There are undoubtedly parallels in Ireland (e.g. Harbison 1969, nos. 17, 348, 350), but it is not clear they are any more numerous there than in Britain.

Sub-class 2D, Type Halberton (Type series nos. 15-19)
When in good condition, as in the type example from Halberton, Devon (no 15; Exeter Museum), this sub-class has near straight sides (RMO < 0.025) and also tends to have less arched butts than on Sub-class 2C. There is also a tendency to have more strongly expanding haft ends (EH ≥ 0.14). Furthermore, none are yet known to have been embellished above the edge bevels or along the sides. Where cutting edge preparation has led to expansion of the blade tips, the resulting out-turn is very small. The explanation may lie in these axes being sharpened more by grinding than by hammering, and such a practice perpetuated throughout use-life could be an important distinction in technological practice. Nevertheless, it has already been mentioned above that Sub-class 2D axes may form a continuous spectrum with those of Sub-class 2C.

There are several trapezoidal Class 2 axes in northern Britain which Schmidt & Burgess place within their Type Growtown/Milton Moss (Schmidt & Burgess 1981, especially nos. 1-3, 5, 7-8, 10, 12, 14-15) and some of these are undoubtedly equivalent to Sub-class 2D. There is probably also a small group amongst the large Irish corpus; possible examples are Harbison (1969) nos. 199, 212, 216, 240, 277, 437, 440, 448, 458, 459, 462, 473, 479, 484, 487, 489. 491, 495 and 503, but these may well include axes with significant outline reduction. The list includes the pair of axes from the Growtown association, Co Meath (*ibid*, nos. 458-9).

Sub-class 2D is important in terms of its potential Continental background. Although they come in varied proportions on the Continent, trapezoidal axes with lenticular profiles are a recurring theme in many regions.

Sub-class 2E, hachettes (Type series nos. 20-21)
Although united by their squatness and small overall size, it is not obvious that this sub-class of very few examples is homogeneous in other key attributes; consequently no type-name has been applied. However, Sub-class 2E can usefully be termed 'hachettes' after the terminology applied to small stone axes on the Continent. This highlights the most plausible form of hafting, in a sleeve first rather than directly into a haft. The only comparable example from northern Britain is poorly provenanced to 'Aberdeenshire' (Schmidt & Burgess 1981, no 276). It is likely that several occur in Ireland (e.g. Harbison 1969, nos. 20, 234, 261, 293, 450, 461, 498) but published details do not always allow discrimination between 2E hachettes and blade fragments (reworked or otherwise) of larger axes. Most of the plausible parallels are unprovenanced, but there is an important definitive occurrence in the Carrickshedoge hoard, Co Wexford (Harbison 1969, no 450; and author's study). Occasional examples of

similar hachettes may also occur on the near-Continent, for example, at Emzen, Saarland (Kibbert 1980, no 37A), Collinée, Côtes d'Armor (Briard 1965, 55 fig. 12.1) and Chapelle-Achard, Vendée (Ferrier & Roussot-Larroque 1971, 84-5 fig 1.3).

Class 3 axes

Class 3 axes continue to feature the neat lenticular profiles of Class 2. However, the combination of the two butt-width ratios – RWB & RWB′ – provides a good separation between the two classes and the fact that in southern Britain this correlates almost completely with the copper/bronze distinction gives it great significance. Since there are no grounds for suspecting any significant hiatus in production or circulation (for example, Ross Island metal is dominant on both sides of the metallurgical transition), it can be argued that the switch in morphology was a deliberate choice tied to the switch in technology (Needham 2004, 236). With rare exceptions, therefore, attribution to Class 3 rather than Class 2 is straightforward.

As with Class 2, a variety of shapes can be discerned within Class 3. Most of the sub-division (that for Sub-classes 3C – 3G) relates to the line of the sides and the attendant effects on body expansion. Sub-classes 3A and 3B, however, are separated on different grounds relating to butt width and cutting edge width respectively.

Sub-class 3A, Types Scunthorpe and Lansdown (Type series nos. 22-25)

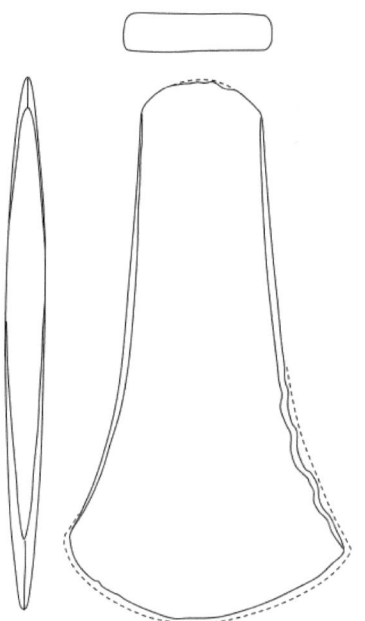

Figure 8: Classic Type Migdale axe from the Migdale hoard, Highland; scale 50%; drawing Stuart Needham

Axes with medium-broad butts (RWB 0.38 – 0.46 and RWB′ 0.21 – 0.29) have been separated out, firstly, because they are morphologically closest to Class 2 axes. Secondly, a high proportion of Schmidt & Burgess's Type Migdale fall within this dimensional bracket (1981, nos. 62 – 190) and it is important to identify the closest parallels in the south given the significance of the Migdale tradition. The present writer has suggested a refinement of Type Migdale in the north, thereby excluding those axes where the butt is narrower and/or the haft-end sides are more divergent, these corresponding more to southern Sub-classes 3C – 3E. The remainder, still forming the majority of Schmidt & Burgess's type, have been referred to as *classic Migdale axes* (Fig 8; Needham 2004, 220). Axes close to Type Migdale in this narrower definition, however, are sparse in southern Britain.

3A Type Scunthorpe: Where Sub-class 3A axes have only gently curving sides which begin to expand slightly almost from the butt, they have been separated as *Type Scunthorpe*, after a find from Morecambe Avenue in that North Lincolnshire town (no 22; Davey 1973, 58 no 2, 59 fig 2.2). These actually look very similar to 2C Type Purdis Farm axes, differing only in having narrower bodies overall. Some of the best parallels in northern Britain are the narrower-butted examples amongst Type Dunnottar (e.g. Schmidt & Burgess 1981, nos. 45-47, 54-55), thus emphasising the typological linkage in this particular axe shape across what is otherwise a bimodal divide within in the whole Class 2/Class 3 spectrum. Other similar northern axes have been placed by Schmidt & Burgess amongst Type Migdale (e.g. nos. 64, 112, 113, 141). Significantly, perhaps, three of those examples cited are from The Maidens hoard, Ayrshire, some distance from the Migdale production heartland of north-east Scotland where classic Migdale axes abound.

3A Type Lansdown: Those axes most similar to the *classic Migdale* type are labelled here *Type Lansdown*, after a find from north-east Somerset (no 24; Dobson 1931, 81, 243-4), thus avoiding confusion with Schmidt & Burgess's looser Migdale definition. They have haft ends which are parallel or expand only minimally, but their curved sides continue to flare all the way to the blade tips, thus still giving rise to a broad mid-blade and a broad cutting edge. It is certainly possible that some or all of Type Lansdown are products of the Migdale heartland metalworking tradition. Occasional axes in Britain (including northern Britain) are characterised by slightly expanded butts which give the body a slightly waisted appearance (type series no 25). These have not been separated as a type, because the expansion is small and variable and may not always have been intentionally produced. They are thus treated as variants of Type Lansdown and Type (classic) Migdale.

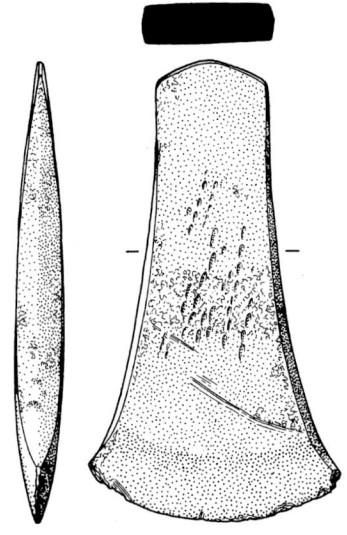

Figure 9: Sub-class 3A Type Scunthorpe axe from a grave at Manor Farm, Lancashire; scale 50%; drawing Phil Dean (after Needham 1987a)

Amongst the abundance of axes metrically comparable to Sub-class 3A in northern Britain are a good number from hoards (e.g. Schmidt & Burgess 1981; Needham 2004). In contrast, there are no associations in the south. The nearest two associations are from graves. The axe from the Butterwick grave, North Yorkshire, corresponds to Type Lansdown (marginally waisted variant), whilst that in the Manor Farm grave, Borwick, Lancashire (Fig 9), corresponds to Type Scunthorpe (Kinnes 1985, A12; Needham 1987a).

Sub-class 3B, Type Boreland (Type series nos. 26-28)
Harbison recognised that one dominant theme amongst the Irish flat axes lacking stop-bevels was the broadening of the cutting edge to proportions not seen on any other Bronze Age axes; he defined them as *Type Killaha*, the cutting edge being more than two-thirds the length of the axe (Harbison 1969, 24). These same proportions were adopted by Schmidt & Burgess (1981, 33) in order to isolate the small number of Type Killaha axes in northern Britain, and again, the present writer found that a bimodal distribution for Class 3 axes split at a comparable value (Needham 1983, fig 156b). In fact, in southern Britain, where broad-edged axes are more numerous than in the north, all those with RWE greater or equal to 0.66 can be confidently attributed to this type. Despite the numerical dominance of the Irish parallels, a British type-name has been applied – *Type Boreland* – after the hoard of two axes from Boreland Farm, Inch, Dumfries & Galloway (no 28; Schmidt & Burgess 1981, nos. 56-57), because there is clear evidence from moulds, including that from Bwlch y Maen, Penmachno, Conwy (Britton 1963, Appendix B I.6, 268 & 321), for production this side of the Irish Sea (Needham 2004, 224). Associations for the type in the south are from Oddington, Gloucestershire (Needham & Saville 1981), possibly Cholsey, Oxfordshire (Rutland & Coghlan 1972, 46-9 nos. 2-3, 47 fig 1) and possibly Easton Cliffs, Reydon, Suffolk[5] (Martin *et al*. 1981, 74 – 'Covehithe'), in all three cases the second axe being of Sub-class 3E.

Axes of Type Boreland are not numerous in Britain, but there is a scatter of finds across much of the island. The contrasting abundance of the type in Ireland suggests that it was a

---

[5] The 3B axe was recovered from a ploughed field above the cliff, 200m from the cliff top, whereas the 3E axe was recovered on a separate occasion from cliff collapse on the beach. Both were found with metal-detectors.

style conceived there and propagated to Britain, where local production took place. Harbison catalogued just over 300 examples, although a number of these need to be excluded as belonging to other types. Several, for example, have relative cutting edge widths which fall short of his own specified threshold (e.g. Harbison 1969, nos. 566, 603, 618, 667, 703, 705, 753, 767) and since most of these have slender parallel haft ends, it may be that they group instead with axes whose RWE values just overlap those for Type Killaha proper (e.g. ibid, nos. 511, 512, 520, 521, 538, 670, 673). There may be a genuine gradation here which needs to be thoroughly examined through fresh study of the Irish series, but it is noteworthy that even those axes currently accepted within Type Killaha have bodies varying between medium-broad and narrow (as seen for example in type series nos. 27 and 26 respectively). Other obviously deviating axes within Type Killaha tend to be squatter with medium-broad butts (e.g. ibid, nos. 526, 560, 565, 567, 597, 614, 633, 706, 717, 728, 729, 748) and although these often have eligible RWE values, their relationship to other Killaha axes needs to be examined. These comments on the Irish corpus are pertinent in giving the background to the smaller British series despite the local production of at least some this side of the Irish Sea.

Sub-class 3C, Type Harlyn Bay (Type series nos. 29-30)
Amongst the axes with more standard cutting edge widths than Type Boreland, some stand out on account of having sides which are only slightly concave and diverge immediately from very narrow butts. Their strong body expansion is best quantified by EH being greater or equal to 0.15; this inevitably leads to fairly wide cutting edges (RWE 0.60 – 0.65) only a little below the threshold to Sub-class 3B. This may be an extreme shape within a wider spectrum, but it was found that most of the small number of examples catalogued in 1983 were from south-west England; moreover, a univalve stone mould from Altarnun, Cornwall (Britton 1963, 267 fig 6), has an axe matrix whose cast blank might well have produced an axe of this form after post-cast working. Butts on the axes are low-arched and cutting edges are shallow.

There are certainly a few finds to add to the 1983 corpus: one comes from East Coulston, Wiltshire (Devizes Museum 100.1980), and five were identified in the Wales and Marches study-corpus of 2015.[6] This shape of axe may not be confined to southern Britain; a few axes in Schmidt & Burgess's corpus have similar body proportions, but tend to out-turn more towards the blade tips (e.g. Schmidt & Burgess 1981, nos. 150, 166, 186, 256); it is possible this relates to different sharpening practices or longer average use-cycles. Again, only a small number of parallels can be identified in Ireland (e.g. Harbison 1969, nos. 557, 766, 774, 780, 785, 799 &1595) where the examples with provenances intriguingly all come from Ulster.

The one known association for the type is that at Harlyn Bay, Cornwall, where the axe was associated with two gold lunulae and a lost 'buckle'-like object (no 30; Smirke 1865; Smirke 1866-7); this offers the obvious type name. Sub-class 3C axes, being essentially trapezoidal, might be seen as descendants of Sub-class 2D copper axes, a relationship potentially mimicking that observed above between 2C Type Purdis Farm and 3A Type Scunthorpe.

Sub-class 3D, Type Barton Stacey (Type series nos. 32-34)
These represent the middle of the spectrum between strongly divergent (3C) to nearer parallel haft ends (3E). Body sides have a gentle curvature and expand modestly over the length of the haft (EH 0.12 – 0.15). Butts are almost always low-arched and cutting edges tend to be quite shallow, repeating the pattern for Sub-class 3C. The type example, from Barton Stacey, Hampshire, assumed some importance in being demonstrated analytically to have been deliberately tin-coated, a phenomenon otherwise only documented on a few Scottish axes (no 33; Kinnes *et al.* 1979).

---

[6] Needham *et al. in prep.*

In southern Britain this type may now be best represented in Wales and the Marches (up to 10 examples) with others a little beyond in Somerset and Wiltshire; only three were recorded from eastern England in 1983. This distribution assumes interest given that the Walleybourne axe mould, Shropshire (Thomas 1972), is most likely to have produced blanks for 3D axes. This axe shape is also represented in northern Britain (e.g. Schmidt & Burgess 1981, nos. 54, 62, 98, 109, 128, 148, 151, 163, 173, 185, 188, 189, 190, 248), although here it is greatly outnumbered by classic Migdale axes. There are undoubtedly a few candidates to match Type Barton Stacey in Ireland (e.g. Harbison 1969, nos. 1392, 1462, 1488, 1497, 1519, 1537, 1627) but it needs to be independently evaluated whether these are just one end of a distribution centred on slightly narrower blades (equivalent to Sub-class 3G here).

Sub-class 3E, Type Brithdir (Type series nos. 35-38)
Although the distinction from Sub-class 3D is not great, axes with more parallel haft ends (EH ≤ 0.11) are treated as a separate group. The minimal expansion of the haft end is compensated for by greater out-swinging of the blade, hence the mid-blade width function (RW3) remains in the same range as for Sub-classes 3C and 3D. Their body shape anticipates that of Sub-class 3F which is shown by associations to belong to a post-Brithdir/Migdale stage. They are the first type to have incipient or low flanges, although these occur on only some of the axes. They are also the first to carry more formalised decorative schemes than the simple side facets, edge-bevel furrows and emergent rain-pattern present on earlier types; even so, such decoration is infrequent at this stage. Butt shapes, although mainly low-arched, now include some higher-arched examples (e.g. type series no 36).

The 3C-3D-3E-3F connecting series should not be read entirely as a chronological sequence, but there are some grounds for seeing Sub-class 3E as late within the Brithdir stage. This may be emphasised by the Brithdir hoard itself, which contains three 3E axes (nos. 35-36) alongside a 'primitive' stop-bevel axe with a comparably broad mid-blade (no 49; Sub-class 4A). Just as 3E axes may be construed as the forerunners of 3F axes, so too 4A should anticipate the more standardised Sub-class 4B. From this perspective it can be seen that the Brithdir hoard contains the progenitors of the two main types of the subsequent Mile Cross Assemblage.

In addition to the Brithdir hoard, Sub-class 3E axes occur in associations from Oddington (no 37), possibly Reydon and possibly Cholsey, in all three cases with a 3B axe (all cited above).

Sub-class 3E axes are widespread in southern Britain and there are close matches in the north amongst Schmidt & Burgess's Type Migdale and its variants (Schmidt & Burgess 1981, nos. 69, 88, 97, 102, 111, 17, 153, 168, 169, 171, 180, 192, 201, 205, 217). These northern parallels may represent one extreme (narrower butt and haft end generally) of the Migdale type and in the light of the other evidence cited above it is likely that this represents a temporal shift. It is difficult to know whether Sub-class 3E axes in the south derive in part from classic Migdale axes. In Ireland too a small number of axes can be identified with corresponding shape and proportions; as for northern Britain, there may be complex interrelationships with regionally specific modal forms.

Sub-class 3F, Type Moot Low (Type series nos. 40-43)
Sub-class 3F sees the narrowing of the whole axe-head, from butt to cutting edge, relative to Sub-class 3E. The narrowing of the blade (as measured by RW3) in particular is seen from associated finds to be part of a wider chronological trend (Needham 2004, 220-2, fig 19.3). Sub-class 3F is, however, distinctive in its very gracile body and yet still rather well flared lower blade. One further feature that sets 3F axes as a group apart from 3E axes is the depth

of the cutting edge – usually very shallow. This transpires also to be a critical feature in relation to the Irish comparanda since close parallels for the body shape in Ireland most often have rather deeper cutting edges. This may be another example of a basic style being accepted in the two islands, but with some subtle and not necessarily conscious variations in detail. The type name, *Moot Low*, is derived from the famous grave find in Derbyshire (no 40; Bateman 1848, 68).

Occasional axes are morphologically intermediate between Sub-classes 3E and 3F, one example being from the probable association from Castle Rising, Norfolk (no 39; Needham *et al*. 1985, A3).

Sub-class 3F has a restricted distribution in Britain relative to most preceding forms. Most finds come from central Britain (Lancashire/Yorkshire/Derbyshire) with another important cluster in northern East Anglia. The Mile Cross hoard, Norfolk, has the type associated with a Sub-class 4B axe (Needham *et al* 1985, A4). Both axes in a hoard or grave group from Highlow, Derbyshire, are probably of Sub-class 3F (Jewitt 1864; Pennington 1877, 51).[7] Two associated finds, however, are more outlying, that from Caerlaverock, Dumfries & Galloway (Yates 1979), where an example was within 0.6m of an axe of Sub-class 3G, and that from Oxwich Bay on the Gower peninsula, where two belonging fragments of a 3F axe were found with the butt fragment of a second axe.

Outside southern Britain the best 3F parallels are Schmidt & Burgess (1981) nos. 203, 216, 234, 243, 247, 316B, 317, 393, with the addition of a large example from Sherriff Hutton, North Yorkshire (Watkin 1987) and an example from Ballawoods, Isle of Man (Megaw & Hardy 1938, 400 no 42). The extraordinarily large axe with very slender haft end from Lawhead Farm, Midlothian (Schmidt & Burgess 1981, no 246 – county incorrectly given as Lanarkshire; O'Connor & Cowie 2001, 226-7) may also best relate to Sub-class 3F in terms of the British series, but another feasible link is to the small minority of Irish Type Killaha axes discussed above on which the haft end has become narrow (e.g. Harbison 1969, nos. 516, 525, 547, 548, 554, 585, 594). The Lawhead axe has a cutting edge width at the bottom end of the Killaha range as defined (RWE 0.66).

There is a good group of Irish axes, numbering at least 50, with the same body shape, but as already noted they tend to have deeper cutting edges than their British parallels. Without re-study of all those in question, precision in this respect is not possible; those with matching or only slightly deeper cutting edges include Harbison (1969) nos. 833, 836, 902, 910, 914, 938, 944, 986, 991, 1044, 1070, 1078, 1095, 1102, 1108, 1116, 1121, 1162, 1188, 1191, 1207, 1211. In terms of decorative schemes, the Irish group seems to hang together and, again, only detailed new study could assess how this group interrelates with adjacent morphologies within that island's corpus. It is of course possible that some of the British finds, especially those with deeper cutting edges, are actually Irish exports. This cannot, however be the total answer because some Sub-class 3F axes bear punched herringbone designs which, at this first horizon of formal designs in late Period 2, is a feature of central Britain (on varied axe types) and is virtually absent from Ireland.

Sub-class 3G, Type Knapton (Type series nos. 44-47)
The only other Class 3 axes in Britain having narrow blades (RW3 < 0.45) differ from Sub-class 3F in having rather broader haft ends, more in line with Sub-class 3E; this gives the axe a very different appearance. Axes accepted within this sub-class in fact have quite varied body widths overall, as illustrated in the type series; further evaluation will be needed to see

---
[7] One of the axes is lost and classification is based on Jewitt's early depiction of it

whether this variation correlates with any other features. The lower blade is only modestly out-turned. The type is named after an axe in excellent condition from Knapton, East Yorkshire (no 46; Schmidt & Burgess 1981, no 220).

There are only a few examples in southern Britain, but rather more in the north (e.g. Schmidt & Burgess 1981, nos. 72, 210, 211, 212, 213, 215, 220, 236, 272, 313, 314, 341; plus one in the Caerlaverock association – Yates 1979). Those listed are mostly within Schmidt & Burgess's variant Biggar of Type Migdale; so too are a few more with similar proportions but haft ends that slightly expand (Schmidt & Burgess 1981, nos. 222, 223, 224, 225, 227, 237). There are undoubtedly axes matching the 3G shape in Ireland, but probably not a great number and, again, some are the variant with straighter, gently diverging sides. Amongst the best candidates, assuming stop bevels have not been obscured or overlooked in the recording, are Harbison (1969) nos. 829, 837, 955, 984, 1081, 1321, 1395, 1402, 1426, 1427, 1572 & 1588.

Just as for Sub-class 3F axes with their comparably narrow blades, associations for Sub-class 3G point to a Mile Cross/Colleonard Assemblage dating. The example from Caerlaverock was with, or very close to, a 3F axe, while those in the Newport hoard (no 44), and the probable Sherburn Carr and Place Newton associations were each with a Sub-class 4B axe (Needham 1979, 286 fig 12; Schmidt & Burgess 1981, nos. 209B & 317A).

Irish Class 3 axes
It is worth a separate comment on the prolific corpus of Irish Class 3 axes. It has been shown above that there are usually parallels to be found there for the types defined for southern Britain. However, for such a simple form (ignoring for present purposes any decoration), there is a bewildering array of detailed shapes in Ireland and any worthwhile classification needs to review them in their own right, independent of external preconceptions. Peter Harbison's groupings have barely scratched the surface and do not even discriminate between some fundamental aspects of flat and low-flanged axes. What is clear thus far is that the relative frequency of types (i.e. shapes) is likely to be very different in Ireland than in Britain and this undoubtedly has implications for production traditions and/or social preferences. That different balance may also mean that small numbers of axes sharing the same basic proportions and shape in the two islands need not necessarily belong to connected populations. With a complex spectrum of shape variation and, moreover, a strong degree of general parallel tracking between the two island traditions, it is entirely feasible that some close similarities will have arisen due to coincidental convergence at the fringes of otherwise distinguishable modalities. For this reason caution should currently be exercised as to whether such similarities necessarily reflect the same type or a linked idea of an acceptable model. A final comment worth making in this context is the repeated discovery that Class 2 and 3 axes of essentially similar shapes in the two islands nevertheless have different trends with respect to depths of cutting edges – in southern Britain this depth always tends to be shallower than for equivalent Irish and, in some cases, northern British implements.

Class 4 axes
When in fair or better surface condition, Class 4 axes are readily distinguishable from Class 3. Even if the stop bevel (which can be a subtle feature) has been erased through surface loss, there is usually a strong indication of its former presence in the lozengic long-profile of the body. Very occasionally even axes in fine condition have a lozengic profile on which the thickest point is *not* marked by a linear bevel and is instead a more rounded change in plane; these are still treated as belonging to Class 4. Where condition is sufficiently good, the great majority of Class 4 axes show evidence for low flanges, but it should not be assumed they

were universally present, particularly on the earlier types (i.e. of the Brithdir and Mile Cross Assemblages).

Class 4 axes overlap the latter half of Class 3 development and then continue beyond (Fig 3). During the period of overlap associations show that relative blade widths are in harmony between the two Classes, RW3 being greater than 0.48 for the late Brithdir Assemblage and mainly between 0.41 and 0.48 for the Mile Cross Assemblage (Needham 2004, fig 19.3). By the Willerby Assemblage, Class 3 axes have disappeared from the British scene and Class 4 have RW3 values mainly below 0.41. These Assemblage-derived boundaries for RW3 therefore assume some importance at a gross statistical level.

A second guiding force in the sub-classification of Class 4 is, yet again, the precise line of the sides; now, however, in addition to the two main factors considered for Class 3 axes (body divergence and side curvature), there are the issues of: i) whether sides are slightly angled at the stop or continue without deflection and, ii) the degree of change in curvature along the length of the side. Most Class 3 axes show relatively little change in side curvature (excluding any blade tip expansion). Amongst Class 4 axes, however, there are strong differences between sides which have the maximum offset around the centre (ASD ~0.50) and those for which it is close to the cutting edge (e.g. ASD 0.80). This longitudinal asymmetry of side curvature produces the familiar 'crescentic' lower blades of some late low-flanged axes and, indeed, their successors – Class 5 axes.

Class 4A, Type Kettering (Type series nos. 48-50)
Relatively few axes (nine are known from southern Britain) are attributed to this sub-class, inclusion being based on broad blades, of a breadth which is consonant with Brithdir Assemblage Class 3 axes (RW3 > 0.48). Such a division cannot be more than statistical, but one associated example, in the Brithdir hoard itself (no 35), supports the dating of the earliest stop bevel axes to that assemblage, although probably to a late stage within it (above). Another association is the grave group at Shuttlestone Plantation, Parwich, Derbyshire; the probable 4A axe (stop bevel obscured by encrustation; no 50) is associated with a Series 2 bronze dagger and a jet disc bead, and bone from the inhumation has been radiocarbon dated 2150 – 1960 cal BC (Needham *et al* 2010, 371; the axe was published there as belonging to Sub-class 4B, but its blade is actually wider).

Further support for an early date might come from the fact that, unlike for Sub-class 4B (below), these axes are not particularly standardised in shape, nor indeed in the way the stop was executed. Most have sides which are more or less angled in the middle, although this can be a rounded angle, as in the type example from Kettering, Northamptonshire (no 48; Crawford 1912, 309). However, an example from Walton Heath, Surrey (Needham 1987b, 98 fig 5.1), has continuously curved sides and, had it lacked a stop-bevel, would lie somewhere between Sub-classes 3B and 3E. The Brithdir example is similar (no 49), but has an unusual stop-bump, a feature also possessed by an axe from the River Avon in Wiltshire (Saunders 1975-6). Another from Wiltshire – The Bake – has strongly diverging, near-straight sides giving a shape not unlike Sub-class 3C (Moore & Rowlands 1972, 51 no 1, pl VI.1). As a group therefore, there are sufficient unusual features to suggest that they represent a stage of experimentation with the idea of adding a stop feature to divide the haft end from the blade.

The angled sides seen on the majority of 4A axes become a characteristic feature on Sub-class 4B. Indeed, it is possible to regard one or two axes in this group which look very close to the latter sub-class – as is the case for the Shuttlestone Plantation example (no 50) – as actually being 4B axes whose blade widths fall at the tail end of a normal distribution for RW3.

Outside southern Britain these broad-bladed stop-bevel axes seem to be rare. One comes from Middleton-on-the-Wolds, East Yorkshire (Schmidt & Burgess 1981, no 310) and another is recognisable in Harbison's corpus (1969, no 514; possibly also no 1345). The latter is otherwise a Type Killaha axe (*cf* Sub-class 3B) and it seems possible that there may have been others in Ireland on which the stop bevel has not been observed or has been lost to deterioration. However, even stop-bevel axes of the succeeding phase (equivalent to Sub-class 4B) are not frequent in Ireland, metalworkers or communities there preferring to develop Class 3 axes instead. One Continental axe seems to be closely related to the 4A experimental type, that in the Wageningen hoard, Gelderland, Netherlands (Butler 1963, 16 fig 1.3; Needham 1983, 160), for it has a distinct transverse bevel (not shown in previously published drawings; Fig 10) associated with a broad blade and a body shape comparable to some of the southern British examples.

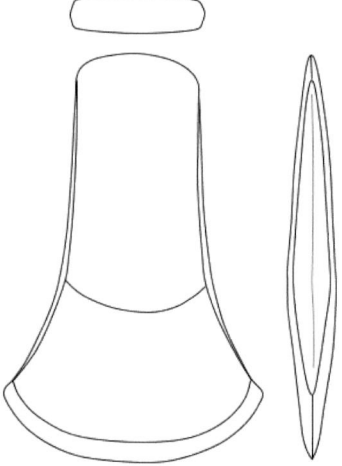

Figure 10: Sub-class 4A-related axe from the Wageningen hoard, Gelderland, Netherlands; scale 50%; drawing: Stuart Needham

Sub-class 4B, Type Aylesford (Type series nos. 51-54)
Sub-class 4B axes are defined as having medium-broad mid-blades (RW3 0.41 – 0.48). The type name is after a rather poorly recorded grave uncovered at Aylesford, Kent; the axe was associated with two daggers (no 53; Piggott 1963, 87 fig 20.1-3; Ashbee 1997, 152-4, fig 1). In contrast to the lack of homogeneity seen amongst Sub-class 4A, axes classified as 4B are more standardised. In most cases the haft end has near-straight sides which diverge slightly or hardly at all. However, in line with the stop (which is now almost invariably a simple bevel) there is usually a distinct change of angle in the sides; alongside the blade the sides expand more widely, either in another near-straight line, or in a gently flaring curve. Although on well-preserved examples the angle is generally obvious, there is sometimes as little as 5° deflection between the stretches immediately above and below the stop. In a small minority of cases there is no deflection level with the stop, the sides instead following a continuous curve from butt to blade tips; these examples are essentially continuing the lines of Class 3 axes and, had they lacked the stop bevel, would not necessarily be distinguishable from one of Sub-classes 3F or 3G. Low flanges are frequent on Sub-class 4B, but not universally present. Cutting edges are generally rather shallow and blade tips barely if at all expanded.

Sub-class 4B axes, like their 3F contemporaries, prove to have a significant regionalised distribution, this time largely restricted to southern Britain. North of the Humber-Mersey line, only a few parallels could be identified in Schmidt & Burgess's corpus (1981, nos. 204, 229, 310, 311, 316C, 317A – some attributed after personal inspection by the present writer). Although those authors define a 'Type Aylesford' to include 18 axes, only four of these meet the present criteria, the others having narrower blades and sometimes sides continuing on to the blade with barely any expansion; indeed, at least two have no stop-bevel. Since their corpus, two important finds of potentially relevant axes have been made in Scotland. Two of the three axes found in a hoard at Dunsapie Crag, Edinburgh, have dimensions corresponding broadly to southern British Sub-class 4B (O'Connor & Cowie 2001, 220-2 nos. 1 & 2). However, that with the better preserved cutting edge (no 1) has well out-turned blade tips uncharacteristic of the southern type; this is in fact a trait of the Irish parallels about to be discussed. Whether the second 4B axe from Dunsapie Crag had the same detail is uncertain. The second find is from Crawhill Farm, Fife, where one of two axes is of Class 4 (Scottish Treasure Trove case 1996/11); severe loss at the cutting edge and butt make calculation of its relative blade width imprecise, but it would appear to be somewhere close to the borderline between 4A and 4B axes as defined here.

Only a small number of stop-bevel axes in Ireland have the medium-broad blade matching Sub-class 4B and these tend to be different in one of two respects; most have out-swinging blade tips like Dunsapie Crag no 1 (above) but unlike southern British 4B axes (Harbison 1969, nos. 812, 1027, 1047, 1050, 1141, 1441, 1514), while others are rather squat axes of proportions only occasionally found amongst the British sub-class (*ibid,* nos. 854, 1201, 1280, 1430). A further axe, excavated from the periphery of the Newgrange passage tomb, Co Meath (O'Kelly & Shell 1979), is different in yet another way – the sides of the haft end curve inwards towards the butt; however, it seems that this axe had not been finished and perhaps its outline shape would have been further modified. Two unprovenanced axes (Harbison 1969, no 1510 and an unpublished piece in Ulster Museum) are much more like the classic southern British form.

Axes of Sub-class 4B occur in several hoards as well as the probable Aylesford grave. Not all are documented associations, but the recurrence of associations with Class 3 axes of Sub-classes 3F and 3G is noteworthy: Mile Cross, Norfolk (no. 52); Newport, Gwent (no 51); Place Newton, East Yorkshire; Sherburn Carr, North Yorkshire. In other cases, two 4B axes are together: St Erth, Cornwall; Hopton Castle, Shropshire. The second axe in the uncertain association from near the Dhustone Quarry, Shropshire (no 54) is a rather later, Class 5 axe (Needham 1979, 279 fig 9.4).

Sub-class 4C, Type Mount Pleasant (Type series 55-57)
This Sub-class is defined as having similar shape properties to Sub-class 4B, but altered proportions, the blade now being narrower (RW3 < 0.41). In this last respect they match the main succeeding type of Class 4 axe (4E) which is the mainstay of the Willerby Assemblage. However, the range for overall side curvature (quantified by RMO) is instead in line with Sub-class 4B. Morphologically, therefore, they can be regarded as intermediate or transitional; this is reinforced by the fact that the asymmetry of the sides (ASD) shows a wide spread of values overlapping both the Mile Cross and the Willerby axe groups. This pattern of connections is summarised in Table 3. There is bimodality in the ASD ratio around a value of about 0.65 for Class 4 axes as a whole, but Sub-class 4C axes seem to present an even spread across the trough.

Table 3: Simplified summary of the critical dimensional interconnections between axes of Sub-classes 4B to 4E

Sub-class	RMO		ASD		RW3	
	< 0.10	> 0.10	< 0.65	> 0.65	> 0.41	< 0.41
4B	X		X		X	
4C	X		X	X		X
4D	X			X		X
4E	X	X		X	x*	X

* Type Glebe Farm

While the mid-blade is narrower than on Sub-class 4B, the lower part of the blade usually swings outwards a little more to maintain breadth at the cutting edge. These shape characteristics can be seen to herald the progressively more out-turning lower blades of Sub-class 4E. The narrowing of the mid-blade on 4C axes also leads to a lessening of the angle at the stop, so this can be an even more subtle inflexion than seen on Sub-class 4B.

Sub-class 4C axes are not known from hoards or graves in Britain. Dating therefore relies heavily on typological considerations and it is assumed they belong close to the Period 2/3 boundary, *circa* 2000 – 1900 BC. One very fine example came from an excavated context at the Mount Pleasant great-henge enclosure, Dorset (Britton 1979), and this is used as the type example (no 56). The well recognised British/Irish export in the Dieskau 2 hoard, Sachsen-Anhalt, Germany (e.g. von Brunn 1959, Tf 16.3; O'Connor 2010), can be attributed to Sub-class 4C (Needham 1983, 174; personal study; Fig 11). Some other Continental finds also relate to this sub-class, but this is not the place for an extended discussion of their significance.

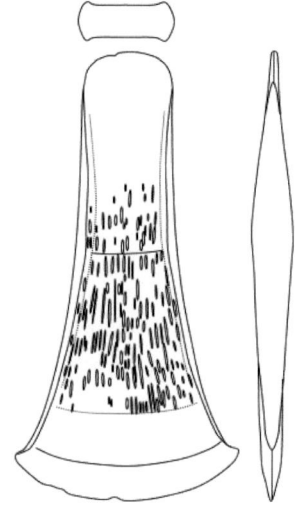

Figure 11: British-Irish low-flanged axe of Sub-class 4C from the Dieskau 2 hoard, Halle, Germany; scale 50%; drawing: Stuart Needham

The sub-class is not very well represented in southern Britain, and axes closely matching the shape further north are equally sparse (e.g. Schmidt & Burgess 1981, nos. 312, 318, 321). There may be more in Ireland in absolute numbers, though not necessarily proportionally (e.g. Harbison 1969, nos. 848, 886, 900, 907, 930, 956, 983, 990, 1010, 1019, 1183, 1287, 1289, 1297, 1319, 1328), and these might grade more imperceptibly into the local Sub-class 4B axes (especially those with out-swinging blade tips) than is the case in Britain. The poor numerical representation of the sub-class in Britain could be seen to support them having been a form in transition between 4B and 4E axes.

Sub-class 4D, Type Cardiff Castle (Type series nos. 58-60)
Several axes in southern Britain have sides which curve asymmetrically (ASD > 0.65), but which are nevertheless not deeply curved (RMO < 0.06); the latter feature is used to distinguish them from Sub-class 4E axes, which share the side asymmetry. For the most part mid-blade width is narrow (RW3 < 0.42). The limited divergence of the lower sides leads to rather narrow cutting edges (RWE < 0.51) and there is often no break in the sides at the stop. On the rarer occasions where there is a slight angle in line with the stop bevel, it is the overall broader body, especially at the haft end, which differentiates them from Sub-class 4C. These are subtle differences and, again, there is probably some gradation between the types. There is also a trend towards deeper cutting edges on 4D axes (RDE > 0.20). The sub-class has been given a type-name after a find from Cardiff Castle (no 60; Savory 1980, 101 no 120, fig 18.120);[8] however, it is not especially homogeneous in its morphology and this might suggest that the southern British examples are imports drawn from a larger repertoire elsewhere.

Axes with these characteristics in northern Britain are equally few and are split between various types and variants in Schmidt & Burgess's scheme (Schmidt & Burgess 1981, nos. 206, 328, 332, 335, 382, 383, 386, 388, 392). In contrast, there is potentially a much larger number from Ireland, even allowing for the possibility that some will have damaged blade tips not clear from the published records; over 50 can be identified from Harbison's corpus and this may be an underestimate.

---

[8] The gently scalloped outline of this example is caused by lozenge faceting of the sides

Whether Sub-class 4D axes represent a distinct trend from the many examples with similar bodies but slightly more out-turned blade tips (i.e. Sub-class 4E), is difficult to say without more detailed analysis. Nevertheless, the less out-turned tips do potentially make these a bridge between earlier Class 4 axes and the prevailing Period 3 fashion for strongly out-turned blade tips, represented by Sub-classes 4E and 4F. Some support for a transitional position comes from associations. A 4D-like axe with a rather diffuse stop-bevel from Knockaun, Co Waterford, was associated with an axe that would be best classified as Sub-class 3G in southern Britain, albeit with a blade width (RW3 0.40) more in line with the Willerby Assemblage (Fig 12; Harbison 1969, nos. 959-960; personal study);[9] both are in fine condition. Another in the Dunsapie hoard mentioned above (O'Connor & Cowie 2001, 220-2 no 3) was instead with two 4B axes of the Irish variant. Both finds suggest origins in the Mile Cross/Colleonard/Ballyvalley Assemblages. One 4D axe, in the Willerby hoard (no. 59), was associated with 4E axes and this is repeated in the Scrabo Hill group, Co Down (Harbison 1969, no 1000), attributable to the Irish equivalent of the Willerby Assemblage. A grave find from Wilsford G64, Wiltshire (Annable & Simpson 1964, no 315), may be a diminutive of this axe form, but it can alternatively be regarded as an axe-chisel (below).

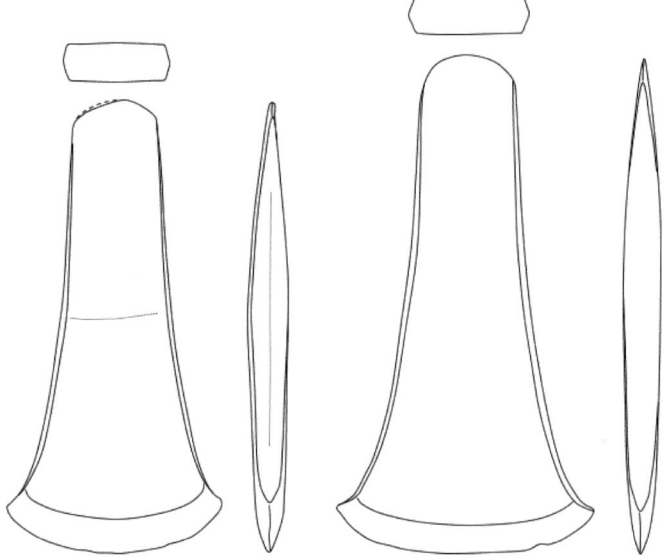

Figure 12: Hoard of two axes from Knockaun, Co Waterford, similar to Sub-classes 4D (left) and 3G (right); note that decoration is not shown; scale 50%; drawings Stuart Needham

The strength of numbers of 4D-like axes in Ireland is probably significant in terms of subsequent evolution there, since one of the dominant shapes amongst Harbison's Derryniggin axes perpetuates the fairly broadly proportioned and near-parallel body, although now associated with more dramatically out-turned lower blades. It is certainly feasible that the British finds of Sub-class 4D axes are mainly Irish imports.

Sub-class 4E, Types Glebe Farm and Whittington (Type series nos. 61-66)
This is the predominant axe shape attributable to the Willerby Assemblage in southern Britain, familiar for its strongly flared lower blades giving a rather 'crescentic' appearance. This not only gives a deep concavity to the sides (RMO > 0.06, and up to 0.15), but also the most extreme asymmetry in side curvature – the maximum offset being close to the blade tips (ASD > 0.65). The strong out-turn of the blade tips, however, springs from a relatively narrow mid-blade, narrower than all preceding axes except Sub-classes 4C and 4D. RW3 is usually less than 0.41 and a handful of examples with slightly greater values might simply be the tail of a normal distribution for this attribute; these have nevertheless been distinguished by their own type name (Type Glebe Farm) because of their greater similarity to antecedent Class 4 axes. The line of the sides on 4E axes now very rarely has any inflexion alongside the stop bevel (although lozenge-facet decoration of the sides can sometimes indent the sides significantly here – e.g. nos. 61, 63 & 65). Instead the body sides sometimes vary in ways little seen earlier, gentle sinuous or bowed lines being added to the previous repertoire of

---

[9] Some Class 3 axes from Ireland have narrower blades than the range found in southern Britain

fairly straight to gently concave sides. The more sinuous-sided axes can result in slight body constrictions which may be at, above or below the stop-bevel; this too can give the appearance of a subtle angle. Bodies are often not far from parallel-sided, but others expand more and thus have echoes of 4C and some 4D shapes. In 1983 four variants were defined to accommodate the main variations noted above; two have been retained here and a third is now defined as Sub-class 4F.

4E Type Glebe Farm (Type series nos. 61-62): Named after a find from Winterbourne Steepleton, Dorset (no. 61; Megaw & Hardy 1938, 299 no. 30), this small minority of axes has relatively broad blades (RW3 > 0.41), hence potentially harking back to pre-Willerby Assemblage forms. In all other respects they match mainstream 4E axes and the alternative possibility raised above is that they represent the tail of a normal distribution of blade widths.

An example with 4E Type Glebe Farm proportions occurs in the Willerby Wold hoard, North Yorkshire; it is attributed by Schmidt & Burgess to their Type Scrabo Hill (1981, no 337), but the haft end is unusually short (proportionally) for any Class 4 axe and the butt tapers abruptly in profile. It is likely this has lost some length at the butt before reworking, in which case its body length (LB) would originally have been greater and relative blade width (RW3) correspondingly less. Type Glebe Farm is not otherwise known from associations.

4E Type Whittington (Type series nos. 63-66): The type find is from Gloucestershire (no 49; Evans 1881, 45-6). This type accounts for the great majority of 4E axes, those conforming to all the key criteria – narrow blades (RW3 < 0.41), asymmetric side curves (ASD > 0.65) with strongly out-turned cutting edges (RMO >0.06). There is variation in the exact line of the body sides; most are straight (no 63-64) or gently concave/angled (no 65), but there are both gently convex (no 66) and more sinuous variants (nos. 67-69). The former variant is occasionally inflected with a slight swelling in line with the stop. The more sinuous side shapes (nos. 67-69) give rise to a slight 'waist', or subtle angle somewhere around the middle of the body, somewhat reminiscent of the body angles on 4B and 4C axes. This particular side line gives rise to fairly narrow mid-blades (RW3) and is associated with only moderate blade tip out-turn (RMO 0.06 – 0.09), hence cutting edge widths (RWE) are also low within the 4E range. It is not clear that sinuosity was an intentional trend and it may sometimes be a by-product of the way in which sides were shaped and decorated.

A small number of 4E Type Whittington axes, including some close parallels in northern Britain and Ireland, are unusually large and tend to bear complex punch-decorated panels. Even so, they are not entirely homogenous in form. The line of the sides is either smooth with little curvature until the lower blade, the typical shape for Sub-class 4E, or slightly angled at the stop as is the case for the illustrated example (no 65; where the angle is further emphasised by the indentations caused by side facets). This example is compared to a newer find from Mosedale House Farm, Cumbria, by Burgess and Richardson (1985, 46). The subtle angling of this latter group makes it rather similar to 4B Type Aylesford axes, some of which are also large in size (e.g. nos. 53-54) and this may be their ancestry.

Parallels will not be listed in detail here since there are a good number in northern Britain including most of Schmidt & Burgess's (1981) Types Glenalla, Falkland, Scrabo Hill and Bandon, and many in Ireland amongst Harbison's (1969) Type Ballyvalley and, to a lesser extent, Type Derryniggin. Schmidt & Burgess recognise a specifically Irish strain in their definition of Type Bandon, but there is an outstanding problem as to how Irish axes of the basic 4E shape might be differentiated from those of classic Derryniggin type, the former presumptively dating to Period 3, the latter to Period 4. Some of the famous British-Irish exports to the Continent are closest to Sub-class 4E. The example in the important Pile hoard, Scania, Sweden (Vandkilde 2017, 61-3), is rather eroded but metrical evaluation suggests it falls somewhere between Sub-classes 4D and 4E.

Sub-class 4F, Type Asterton Prolley Moor (Type series nos. 70-73)
A small number of axes match Sub-class 4E Type Whittington in all but having unusually narrow bodies; the body is narrow from butt to mid-blade and can be most simply defined by RW3 < 0.32, although MRW is obviously also low for the sub-class (< 0.81). Cutting edge widths tend also to be narrow, although only in one case (Bush Barrow) is RWE low enough to fall, strictly speaking, within the axe-chisel range (below). While it is possible that these axes represent a statistical tail of the 4E distribution, it is significant that they include some funerary finds, mostly being diminutive axes. There are other signs of 'specialisation'. None bear formal decoration, and yet they are very finely crafted. Indeed, the example from the Bush Barrow grave (no 73), Wiltshire, is not only the most slender-bodied of the group, but is also exceptionally thin throughout with tiny, crisp flanges. On the other hand, the type-find from Asterton Prolley Moor (no 70; Phillip 1893), Shropshire, potentially also from a funerary context, is unusually thick for its size.

Sub-class 4F axes are rare; only seven or eight examples were identified from southern Britain before 1983. Class 4 implements of closely comparable shapes may not be frequent in Harbison's Irish corpus either.

No Sub-class 4F axes are known from hoards and instead grave finds provide their chronology. Those at Bush Barrow, West Overton, both Wiltshire, and Breach Farm (no 72), Vale of Glamorgan, are from grave groups datable to Period 3. Moreover, the latter two finds have associated radiocarbon measurements of 2020 – 1770 cal BC and 2020 – 1690 cal BC (95% probability) respectively; at 68% probability they are 1950 – 1780 and 1920 – 1755 cal BC (Needham et al 2010, 369).

Class 5 axes (Long-flanged axes; Arreton and allied types)
Class 5 axes are straightforwardly defined on the basis of having relative flange heights (RHF) greater than 0.015 (see above); the maximum absolute flange height should not be less than about 1.5 or 2mm. Early Bronze Age forms of flanged axe are most familiar as the previously defined *Arreton type* (Britton 1963, 284-5), but the Class 5 definition allows in others that fall outside the normally accepted parameters of that type. The flanges extend more or less the full length of the body, from near the butt to well down the blade (although not all the way to the blade tips) – hence the term *long-flanged axes*. Long-flanged axes continue into the early part of the Middle Bronze Age, most notably in the form of *stop-ridge flanged axes* (nomenclature varies) first defined by Sprockhoff (1941, 50; also Butler 1963, 45; Rowlands 1976, 24-7; Schmidt & Burgess 1981, 89-90). These are not considered here. They often differ only subtly in outline shape from Class 5 axes, but may most easily be distinguished by a stop-ridge or stop-ledge, stop forms that are rare on British Early Bronze Age flanged axes.

The rectangularity of body section ratio (RBS) provides a useful additional, albeit less clear-cut, differentiation between Class 4 and Class 5 axes. Bodies on the later class are significantly thicker for the same width (measured in the middle of the body). The peak of the RBS distribution for Class 5 falls in the range 0.40 – 0.55, whereas that for Class 4 is 0.25 – 0.40 (Fig 13). The tails of the two distributions do however overlap, so RBS values alone do not fully discriminate.

Class 5 axes have quite varied body shapes, some of which can be matched within Sub-classes 4C-4F. In the 1983 classification scheme two aspects of body shape – overall body width (MRW) and degree of body expansion (EB) – were used in combination to define six body-shape trends. On later reflection, the differences in body expansion seem to be relatively unimportant visually, whereas differences in overall body width are more obvious from one end of the spectrum to the other. Moreover, this latter attribute can be related to inter-regional connections and intra-regional traditions. The broader bodied axes are not common but tend to have a more inland distribution than Class 5 in general. The narrow-bodied forms find their best parallels in northern France, where the Arreton-parallel *Muids type* seems overall to have narrower bodies than Class 5 in southern

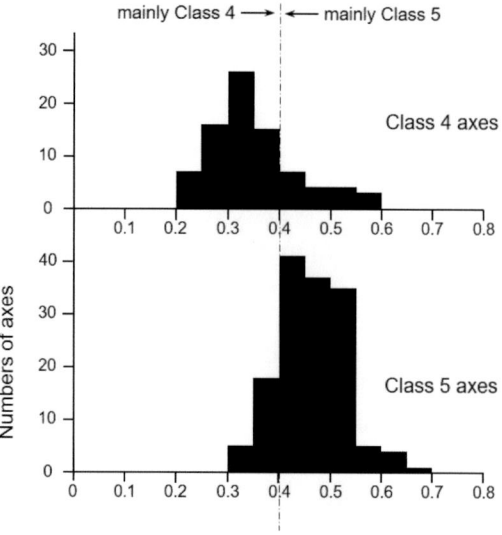

Figure 13: Distribution of rectangularity of body section values (RBS) for Class 4 and 5 axes (after Needham 1983, 141)

Britain; nevertheless, it is not implied that the narrower bodied examples are imports. Another inter-regional connection is provided by axes with the narrowest cutting edges for the class overall. These have been allied with flanged axes of very similar proportions, but sometimes local styling, in northern Europe (Needham 1979, 275-6 – there termed 'squat parallel bodied flanged axes'). The previous six-fold sub-division of Class 5 has thus been abandoned in favour of five new sub-classes, three of which are defined on relative body width, the other two on other features – rather low flanges (5A) and narrow blades (5B).

Most Class 5 axes combine features that are individually frequent amongst the whole corpus. However, some more unusual features occur on small numbers. While butts are most often low-arched to well-arched, very occasionally they can have a more pointed shape (Type series nos. 83 & 87). Straight or indented butts are usually due to damage and/or reworking. Alongside the body the sides vary typically from gently concave to straight to gently convex, but can also be gently S-shaped. A handful of axes even have a convex inflection, or swelling, in line with the stop (no 88). Even fewer are waisted, such that the body is narrowest at a point below the butt (no 89), and this may represent no more than an extreme in the spectrum of concave side shapes.

The flanges as seen in side view are usually described as leaf-shaped. This is often a fair description, although the 'leaf' can be either symmetrical end to end, or broadest somewhere within the haft end. A frequent nuance of the leaf shape has a minor inflexion around the middle which separates a convexly-curved haft end from a more straight-tapered or even concave-tapered blade end (e.g. nos. 75, 83, 85, 87). Occasionally flanges are sub-lozenge shaped (nos. 81, 84). Rarely is the maximum breadth in the blade end and, where this is the case, it can sometimes be argued to result from significant truncation and reworking of the blade (e.g. no 95).

The archetypal blade form is that of a strongly expanded lower blade. Even so, the degree and nature of that expansion varies; in a minority of cases the blade corners are *recurved*, such that the tip itself is swept back beyond a line transverse to the blade's axis (nos. 77, 81, 83, 85, 89, 94, 96). Occasional examples (in good condition) show that the tips had been carefully shaped with squared-off rather than pointed ends (no 85). Morphologically opposite to the recurved form are a few blades that were deliberately expanded in a straight, fan-like flare (nos. 90-92); these are placed in Sub-class 5D Type Staunton.

The stop feature on Class 5 axes is most often a stop-bevel – straight, curved or, rarely, angled (e.g. no 94). The small number of exceptions – in the form of low stop-bumps, stop-ledges or stop-ridges none of which ever reach the height of the flanges (e.g. nos. 81, 90-91, 93, 96, 97) – may anticipate the feature more regularly seen on succeeding flanged axe types of the early Middle Bronze Age. One recurrent feature on Class 5 axes is the butt groove. This runs along the top of the arched butt; it has variable definition, may be slightly wavy or straight, and is sometimes broken in the middle rather than continuous. It has been interpreted as a residual feature formed during post-cast thinning of the butt after a casting jet has been snapped off (Fig 14; Needham 1983, 449-51, fig 198).

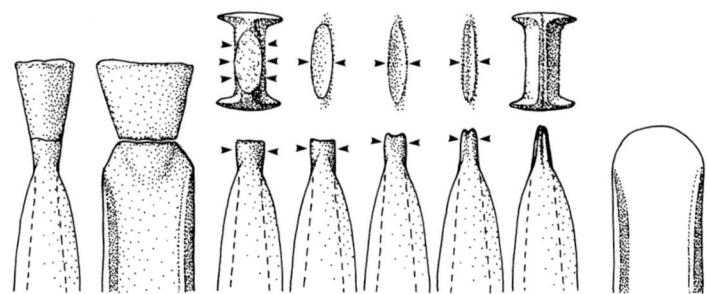

Figure 14: Suggested mode of butt-groove formation on Class 5 axes (after Needham 1983, fig 198)

British finds of Irish Type Derryniggin and allied axes (which are few) conform well enough to Class 5 to be classified thus in the first instance providing flange heights are great enough to satisfy the definition. The Irish corpus of early long-flanged axes needs independent evaluation and will doubtless prove to contain its own sub-classes and to require distinct type-names. One issue in the absence of analysis is that it is not clear whether overall flange-height distribution will be bimodal in the Irish corpus and there may need to be a different basis for differentiating the Irish equivalents of Class 4 and Class 5 axes. However, where there are sufficient grounds for identifying British finds specifically as Irish imports or heavily Irish-influenced, they may be designated for the time being as *Class 5 Irish styles* (Type series nos. 96-97).

Flange height on southern British axes has already been discussed in order to separate Class 5 from Class 4. The variation in relative flange height within this class is however large, from 0.015 to 0.07, and it is possible that there was a tendency for flanges to increase in height during the lifetime of the Arreton Assemblage. Some support for this comes from associated groups of axes; although any single association has a span of values, the average RHF for them ranges from 0.028 to 0.053. This is more likely to be of temporal than other significance. Needless to say, flange heights for individual axes can only be meaningful when used statistically. Nevertheless, it has been considered worthwhile to define one sub-class on the basis of very low flange heights within the Class 5 range.

Sub-class 5A, Type Horncastle (Type series nos. 74-77)
A small number of axes have flanges that are relatively low for the class, RHF between 0.015 and 0.025 (Fig 5) with the maximum flange height being no more than 2mm. Of the 1983 corpus, only seven axes and three possible additions in less certain surface condition conform to this sub-class. With one broad-bodied exception they have medium-broad bodies and butts

are low-arched to moderately arched; blade tips are well expanded or, in one case, recurved. The eponymous find is from Lincolnshire (no 74; Davey 1973, 58 no 20, 61 fig 3.20). Axes in poor condition would not normally be attributed to this sub-class since flange height is often disproportionately reduced relative to axe length; flaking and powdering of flange crests can easily result in the loss of 0.5mm or more in height.

The importance of isolating this group is that they may be particularly early examples of the class, representing a phase when the average height of flanges was being quickly increased from the low flanges of Class 4. Body shapes correspond well to preceding Sub-classes 4E and 4F axes (Fig 16). Another possibility needs to be kept in mind, namely that they may relate more closely to contemporary Irish axes, for these mostly have lower flanges than on British Class 5. There are certainly some axes in northern Britain which satisfy the criteria for Sub-class 5A; of those studied by the author, examples from Staxton, North Yorkshire, and Brough-under-Stainmore, Cumbria, are good (Schmidt & Burgess 1981, nos. 406 & 411). Careful measurement of flange heights and evaluation of condition would be necessary to confirm other potential candidates amongst their Types Bandon and Balbirnie, some of which probably have low enough flanges to qualify as Class 4 in the current scheme and others of which have the more typical flange heights for Class 5.

One 5A axe comes from the Westbury upon Trym hoard, Avon, and another comes from the Moon's Hill hoard, Isle of Wight (no 77). In both cases the associated axes also have relatively low flanges and these hoards probably fall early within the Arreton tradition (see above). A more recent associated find which may contain relevant axes is from Hackford, Norfolk (West 2014); all three Class 5 axes seem to have low enough RHF values. These, however, have narrower bodies than Sub-class 5A representatives thus far, MRW between 0.70 and 0.81. A fourth axe, of non-British type, was said to have been found a short distance away from these three, but the best parallels in central Europe are dated to a later horizon than would apply to an early stage in the Arreton Assemblage. Even more recent is a hoard from Llanover, Monmouthshire (Gwilt & Lewis 2015), containing three axes which all have relatively low flanges; two of them probably qualify as Type Horncastle as defined.

Sub-class 5B, Types Ashford, Maidenhead and Greengate (Type series nos. 78-81)
This sub-class encompasses the axes characterised by relatively narrow cutting edges which have parallels across the southern North Sea and Channel mentioned above. The RWE distribution for all Class 5 axes appears to be unimodal with a peak between 0.5 and 0.6; on the basis of this attribute alone, this sub-class could represent the arbitrary truncation of the lower tail of a normal distribution. However, there are other features that unite almost all the examples. They are almost always rather small implements with near-parallel sided bodies, the sides only swinging outwards low on the blade. The edge bevels are often relatively deep and encroach on the bottom end of the flanges to form triangular facets. Finally, most have relatively high flanges (RHF > 0.045) and while in theory this might be a distributional shift caused by the shortness of the axes, it has been shown that comparably small axes of other sub-classes within Class 5 have a quite different RHF distribution weighted towards lower values (Needham 1983, 202-3, fig 162b).

That this sub-class is not straightforwardly just one end of a shape spectrum is further suggested by two points. Firstly, very few larger axes in the corpus have such narrow cutting edges (RWE < 0.50) and they do not look like larger versions of 5B implements. Secondly, the more typical Class 5 cutting edge widths (RWE > 0.50) can be found not only on medium to large size axes, but also on a number of small ones. There is then the distinct possibility that there are two overlapping morphological populations amidst Class 5. In suggesting this it does not mean there is no blurring between the two, potentially both at the production stage and in the course of reworking. Significant hammer reworking of the narrower cutting edges of Sub-class 5B axes would generally tend to broaden them, thereby causing some overlap with other sub-classes.

Given these circumstances, plus the fact that it takes only a little variation in the expansion of the blade tips to have a noticeable effect on the RWE value calculated, it has not been thought appropriate to set a harsh boundary in this variable. In addition to the descriptive elements given above, the guidelines adopted are as follows. The core type comprises almost all Class 5 axes shorter than 115mm in length *and* with RWE ≤ 0.50; where RWE falls between 0.51 and 0.54, axes can be included if they are equally short and look similar in form. The aggregate group largely comprises medium-bodied axes, but this is not a defining feature. Two variants have been separated from the main group, which will be described first.

5B Type Ashford (nos. 78-79): This type, named after a find from Kent (no 78; Grove & Terry 1949, 143, 144 fig 2), forms the core of the sub-class and is rather homogeneous. They are all less than 110mm long and can be much smaller (no 79). Up to thirty examples were recorded in the 1983 corpus, mainly distributed around the coastal counties from Norfolk to Devon. One occurs on the south Welsh coast at Margam (Vale of Glamorgan; Savory 1980, fig 18 no 122) and occasional others reach inland to Cambridgeshire and Shropshire. The type does not occur further north in Britain. Neither is it obvious in Ireland, where axes that meet the metrical criteria almost always have the low flanges and the distinctive look of Type Derryniggin and allied (yet to be defined) types.

Axes of similar size and with similar proportions and features have been noted in northern Germany, Denmark, the Low Countries and northern France (Needham 1979, 275-6; Needham 1983, 238-45). The Danish examples are treated by Vandkilde as Type Oldendorf, a type originally defined by Kibbert for Middle West German material (Vandkilde 1996, 117-21; Kibbert 1980, 137-50), but otherwise the detailed styling varies regionally suggesting a shared tradition with regional zones of production traversing the Channel and the southern North Sea.

Several axes occur in certain or possible associations. Most important of these is the Moon's Hill hoard, Isle of Wight, where four examples were associated with three more Class 5 axes, three daggers and three spearheads (Sherwin 1942). The Moon's Hill hoard has been argued to date fairly early in the Arreton Assemblage (Needham 1983, 304). One Type Ashford axe occurs in the Plymstock hoard, Devon (Hawkes & Smith 1955, GB. 9 no 12), which also contains a 5B Type Maidenhead axe amongst many others, and another may have been found with a 5B Type Greengate axe at Salhouse, Norfolk (Norfolk Museum Service 1977, 20, 28).

5B Type Maidenhead (no 81). These are slightly heavier implements than Type Ashford and extend the size range up to 115mm long. They have medium-broad bodies and, rarely for Class 5, are characterised by stop-bumps instead of stop-bevels. Only four were recognised in southern Britain by 1983, two of them being poorly provenanced: 'Norfolk' (no 81) and uncertainly to Mildenhall, Suffolk. An axe from Maidenhead, Berkshire, lacking a few millimetres at the butt, is taken as the type-find (Birmingham Museum, accession no 32'66) and the fourth, from the Plymstock hoard, Devon, is badly damaged around the cutting edge Hawkes & Smith 1955, GB. 9 no 15). Although these two are incomplete, they can confidently be attributed to the type. A second axe in the Plymstock hoard is similar but rather broader-bodied and is classified as 5E (cf 5B) (no 95).

The writer is not aware of any examples of Type Maidenhead in northern Britain. However, there are several good parallels amongst Continental Type Oldendorf (e.g. Kibbert 1980, nos. 202, 204, 212, 218, 250, 256, 260, 261, 265) and it is possible that the British finds are imports from across the southern North Sea.

5B Type Greengate (no 80): Four very small examples have slender bodies, MRW <0.81, while flanges tend to be low. They come from northern East Anglia and North Lincolnshire, the type-find being from Greengate, Swanton Morley, Norfolk (no 80; Norfolk Museum Service Records, Co. no. 15278). Another find of this type is from Barnoldswick, Lancashire (Craven Museum, Skipton) and there are four reasonably good parallels amongst the Irish corpus (Harbison 1969, nos. 1506, 1827, 1879, 1924). None of the type are from secure associations, although one from Salhouse, Norfolk, was likely associated with a 5B Type Ashford axe (Norfolk Museum Service 1977, 20, 28).

The narrowness of the cutting edges of Sub-class 5B axes in general recalls those seen in Class 3 and 4 axe-chisels (below), but they are rarely as narrow (i.e. RWE < 0.45) and the axe-chisel label has therefore been avoided. Moreover, the similarity of Sub-class 5B to a good number of axes on the near-Continent suggests this may not simply be an internal evolution. This cross-sea connection ties in with the extreme south-easterly distribution of Sub-class 5B.

Sub-class 5C, Type Bisham (Type series nos. 82-84)
These axes have the most slender bodies amongst Class 5, MRW < 0.81. The type-find is from the River Thames at Bisham (no 83; Berkshire/Buckinghamshire border; Megaw & Hardy 1938, 277 fig 5a, 299 no 11). There are subtle variations in the shape of the bodies, but this is for the most part a remarkably homogeneous group. Relative flange heights spread through the whole Class 5 range, but are weighted distinctly towards the lower half (RHF <0.035). Two axes have marginally waisted bodies with potential connections to Continental flanged axes (Needham 1979, 278; Needham 1983, 212-3), but these do not as yet merit a separate sub-classification; they are interpreted as having been influenced by Continental styles rather than being imports. A lost axe provenanced to Norton Fitzwarren, Somerset, has an extremely narrow body and correspondingly narrow cutting edge (RWE 0.39; Colquhoun 1978, 85 no 9, 86 fig); it is more likely to be of a Continental type than a variant within the insular Class 5 repertoire.

Sub-class 5C axes also have a more general link across the Channel, because a high proportion of the north French Arreton-like axes – *Type Muids* – are similarly slender-bodied (Blanchet & Mordant 1987 – here mixed in with stop-ridge flanged axes). The Continental link is again emphasised by an overwhelmingly south-eastern distribution in Britain. Examples beyond central and southern England are extremely rare: one in the Menai Bridge hoard, Anglesey, and one from Whittington Fell, Northumberland. Again, few equivalent axes come from Ireland and only a couple are close enough to be considered the same type (Harbison 1969, nos 1850 & 1894) whilst one or two others are distinguished by a deeper cutting edge.

This sub-class is very well represented in Arreton associations. There is one example in each of the Arreton, Buckland, Grunty Fen, Milverton and Moon's Hill hoards, two in each of the Combe Hill, Holywell Row and Poslingford Hall hoards, and four in the Plymstock hoard. Together these hoards probably span the whole of the Arreton phase.

Sub-class 5D, Types West Drayton and Staunton (Type series nos. 85-92)
Sub-class 5D axes are those with medium-broad bodies, MRW between 0.81 and 1.0. This is the most common sub-class accounting for around half of Class 5. Most of these axes are noticeably chunkier in the body than Sub-class 5C, but there is little else to differentiate them in terms of specific features. Body sides above mid-blade range from very gently concave to near-straight to marginally convex. An extreme version of the convex end of the spectrum is seen in four axes with a slight swelling or inflexion in line with the stop (no 88; other examples are more subtly inflected). Similarly, two or three of the concave-sided examples expand fractionally at the butt to give a slightly waisted body (no 89). The only variation given a separate type-name, however, involves the combination of particular blade shape and stop form (Type Staunton).

Unlike the flange height distribution (RHF) seen for Sub-class 5C, that for Sub-class 5D is evenly spread through the full Class 5 range and this suggests that over the course of the Arreton Assemblage more substantial bodies gained favour at the expense of slender ones.

5D Type West Drayton: The type-find for the great majority of 5D axes is from West Drayton, Greater London (no 86; Megaw & Hardy 1938, 300 no 56). These have the standard 'crescentic' form of lower blade with moderately deep cutting edges and well expanded blade tips, a reasonable number of which are recurved (nos. 85 & 89). Type West Drayton is less homogeneous than Type Bisham, even with the variant shapes noted above having been excluded from the type. No coherent internal trends have been identified by the writer but, should any be perceived in the future, additional type names can be applied.

Being the dominant type of Class 5 axe, these appear in most contemporary hoards and area finds: there is one example each at Buckland, Combe Hill, Ebnal, Pilsdon, Thornton Carrs and Totland, two at Holywell Row, Milverton and Westbury upon Trym, three at Arreton Down, and as many as six at both Plymstock and Poslingford Hall.

This is primarily a southern British type, most densely found between Devon and Norfolk/Lincolnshire, but unlike Sub-class 5C it is scattered further to the west and north. There are several examples from Yorkshire with a thinner spread through Wales, north-west England and Scotland. Several also occur in Ireland.

5D Type Staunton: Four axes differ from Type West Drayton in having fanned blades – a straight-flared, steadily expanding lower blade combined with a deep cutting edge. They are not an especially homogeneous group, although two of them have stop-bumps/stop-ribs which are otherwise rare in the class. They justify a type-name (after a find from Staunton, Gloucestershire; no 90; Hart 1967, 11, pl VIIb) because they appear to anticipate or imitate the fanned blade form characteristic of Type Bannockburn, conventionally dated to the earliest Middle Bronze Age (Schmidt & Burgess 1981, nos. 426-440). Type Bannockburn is also characterised by low stop-ribs. One Type Staunton axe was associated with a Sub-class 5C Type Bisham axe at Grunty Fen, Cambridgeshire (no 91). This is a fairly late Arreton hoard to judge from the relative flange heights of the two axes.

Aside from the eponymous example, finds are from the east – Northamptonshire, Cambridgeshire and Norfolk. Closely matching examples in the Irish corpus are rare, the best candidates being Harbison (1969) nos. 1804, 1808 & 1898. In the northern British corpus, one attributed to 'Scotland' (Schmidt & Burgess 1981, no 400) may conform if it is not already a full-blown Type Bannockburn axe.

Sub-class 5E, Types Clifton and cf 5B (Type series nos 93-95)
The final sub-class covers a modest number of axes with relatively broad bodies, MRW >1.0. Again, aside from the altered body proportions, there is little *en masse* to distinguish these from Sub-classes 5C and 5D.

5E Type Clifton: This type embraces the majority of Sub-class 5E which follow the dominant outline patterns seen for Sub-classes 5C and 5D, the two sides obviously just a little further apart. The type-find is from Clifton, Nottinghamshire (no 93; Needham 1979, 268 fig-3.2, 272). A single unprovenanced example (Spalding Gentlemen's Society collection), however, deviates in having the fanned blade of Sub-class 5D Type Staunton; it also has a slightly emphasised stop-bevel and could alternatively be considered a broader variant of that type. Three examples of Type Clifton come from the Plymstock hoard (no 94).

5E (cf 5B): Three axes are more like broader versions of Sub-class 5B but have too wide a cutting edge to be comfortably accommodated within that type. One example comes from the Plymstock hoard (no 94; Hawkes & Smith 1955, GB. 9 no 14). Heavy reworking of blades after damage might account for the form of these axes, in which case their original type would not be assessable.

Sub-class 5E has an interesting distribution relative to all other Class 5 axes, indeed, it is near complementary to those of Sub-classes 5B and 5C. In the corpus area they come almost entirely from a band from the south-west peninsula, via Somerset, Wiltshire and Leicestershire to Nottinghamshire and Norfolk. A single example comes from the Isle of Wight, but otherwise they are absent from south-east England. Two admissible examples are known from Wales (Savory 1980, 166 no 118; AC-NMW 80.60H) and there may be occasional examples from northern Britain (Schmidt & Burgess 1981, nos. 355?, 404, 421 & 514). Two further Scottish finds have a decidedly Derryniggin look, but since there are also resemblances between certain Irish axes (e.g. Harbison 1969, nos. 1693, 1725, 1820, 1867, 1884, 1902, 1953, 1963, 1972) and examples within Sub-class 5E, there may prove to be a complicated spectrum of relationships in this direction.

Flat and low-flanged axe-chisels
Flat and low-flanged axes come in a wide range of sizes, including some of rather diminutive size that could only have functioned at the practical level as fine woodworking tools. Nevertheless, many broadly respect the various forms of their 'standard-size' counterparts and are classified correspondingly. Rather distinct, however, are implements which are not only small, but are also significantly narrower, proportionally, throughout the body and right to the cutting edge; they combine an axe-like haft end with a more chisel-like blade. These are conveniently termed *axe-chisels*, a term which distinguishes them from more conventional *narrow-tanged chisels* (Needham 1983, 254-9). Axe-chisels are most easily recognised from the low values for RWE, a maximum of around 0.45 and often much less; they are also small – rarely over 100mm long and often much smaller. A few similarly small implements with RWE values between 0.45 and 0.50 – the lower tail of the distribution for Class 4 axes – might be considered to fit better in this category than as diminutive axes; for example, the tiny example from Wilsford G64 noted above under Sub-class 4D. Very delicate side flanges are occasionally present. Axe-chisels can be grouped into three main forms which can be related broadly to contemporary axe types; they cannot be linked stylistically to individual axe sub-classes because of their distinctively narrow proportions.

Class 3 axe-chisels (Type series nos 98-100)
Some axe-chisels have lenticular profiles without any stop-bevel, thus corresponding with Class 3 axes.[10] Because the blade and cutting edge are narrow by definition, there is little scope for variation in the line of the sides, which are straight to marginally concave. Such implements are rare in Britain, but may be a little better represented in Ireland. Harbison's corpus has at least 15 potential examples (1969, nos.1248. 1275, 1355, 1356, 1384, 1484, 1485, 1521, 1522, 1569, 1576, 1613, 1632, 1641, 1646, 1651). Schmidt & Burgess's corpus only has four (1981, nos. 287, 288, 291, 294C?), but two of these are from an important association – The Maidens hoard, Ayrshire – belonging to the Migdale Assemblage. Of equal importance is a newer discovery of a Class 3 axe-chisel with a Sub-class 3D axe, thus of the contemporary Brithdir Assemblage, at Coity Higher, Bridgend (Gwilt et al. 2015).

Class 4B/C axe-chisels (Type series nos. 101-104)
Axe-chisels with lozengic profiles created by a stop-bevel can be divided into two groups. Implements in the first show a distinct inflexion between the haft end and the blade, this despite the limited curvature of the sides possible within the axe-chisel definition. Most in this group, including a later find from Broad Town, Wiltshire (Clarke 2000), are slender, rather homogeneous implements. However, an example from Firle, East Sussex, is relatively squatter and is distinguished by double-bowed sides although the exact shape may have been a little modified by corrosion and subsequent filing (no 102).

The angling of the sides recalls that most frequently encountered on Sub-class 4B and 4C axes and, in the absence of any closely dated associations, it must be assumed that they are broadly contemporary with those types. This is supported by the Llanddyfnan grave group, Anglesey, where a heat-contorted axe-chisel (no 104) can nevertheless be reasonably confidently attributed to Class 4B/C and is associated, with a bronze knife, a narrow-tanged chisel and a Food Vessel Urn (Savory 1980, no 334). A date in later Period 2 seems likely.

Class 4D/E/F axe-chisels (Type series nos. 105-110)
The second lozenge-profile group instead has sides which continue unbroken from haft end to blade, parallel or only slightly diverging; they then swing outwards to greater or lesser degree for the lower blade giving a side shape reminiscent of Sub-class 4D to 4F axes. Despite being infrequent finds, they are very varied in their overall proportions. In addition to the diverse illustrated examples, one from Feltwell, Norfolk, is very squat with S-shaped sides and dished haft-end faces – more exaggerated than no 108. Further variability is introduced on one axe-chisel by the addition of side loops (no 109) and on another by perforated mid-side swellings (no 110).

Only a few southern British examples of Class 4 axe-chisels were recorded in the 1983 corpus, to which can be added one northern find from Ickornshaw, West Yorkshire (Schmidt & Burgess 1981, no 379) and a subsequent find from Warburton, Greater Manchester (no 105; information – Nick Herepath) with a very slender body and overall shape not unlike the larger axe from Bush Barrow (no 73) placed in Sub-class 4F. Likewise, there appears to be only a handful of examples from Ireland (Harbison 1969, nos. 935, 1156, 1251, 1324, 1366, 1449, 1539; plus an example in Ulster Museum from Balleymoney, Co Antrim).

---

[10] Since examples known to the author seem always to be of bronze rather than copper, they have been allied with Class 3 rather than Class 2.

Other chisels and stakes of the Early Bronze Age
In order to prevent uncertainty over the identification of axe-chisels, I will describe other forms of chisel datable to the Early Bronze Age (none are known in Chalcolithic contexts, or in unalloyed copper).

Narrow-tanged chisels (Type series nos. 111-113)
This is the simplest form of chisel, a narrow tang allowing the metal component to be slotted into a morticed handle of wood, bone or antler. It is not a type exclusive to the Early Bronze Age and only those in secure contexts, which are scarce, are therefore covered here. Despite the simplicity of form, shape can vary. The example from a grave at Collingbourne Kingston G4, Wiltshire, is short and has a slight shoulder between blade and tang (no 113; Annable & Simpson 1964, no 387). It is important in having its antler handle surviving. Longer-tanged examples lacking any inflexion between tang and blade come from two other graves, at Froxfield, Hampshire (no 111; Gerloff 1975, pl 53F.2), and Llanddyfnan, Anglesey (no 112; Savory 1980, 199 fig 51 no 334:2), the latter associated with an axe-chisel (no 104). Their respective lengths are very different: Froxfield is 56mm long, Llanddyfnan 110mm.

On the basis of their associations, all three of these grave groups could date to around Period 3 at the latest. The axe-chisel at Llanddyfnan is the most chronologically diagnostic object in association (see above).

Bar-chisels, or stakes (Type series 114-118)
Bar-chisels likewise have a chronology extending beyond the period covered here and only a few examples are known in Early Bronze Age contexts. Most complete is the fine example in the Westbury upon Trym hoard, Avon (no 114; Grinsell 1968, 36 no 50, 52 fig 6), a square-sectioned bar furnished with two opposing lugs. The lugs are unusually placed on the faces rather than the sides. A similarly sectioned bar-chisel from the Plymstock hoard, Devon (no 115; Hawkes & Smith 1955, GB. 9 no 21), has probably lost its butt end, so it cannot be known whether it too was lugged.

Other Early Bronze Age bar-chisels have a more rectangular section, but the more complete examples are side-lugged. Although there may be a reduction in width above the lugs, the 'tang' end is still substantial. The lost example from the Ebnal hoard, Shropshire (no 116; Burgess & Cowen 1972, 170 fig 1.5), appears to have had its blade end missing, but one in a grave at Balneil, Dumfries & Galloway, is intact (no 117; Burgess & Cowen 1972, 174 fig 5). Another Scottish find came from a grave at Carwinning Hill, North Ayrshire (Cowie 1977). Back in southern Britain, a grave at Stanton Moor T3 (interment B), Derbyshire (no 118; Heathcote 1930, 32-8; Longworth 1984, 177 no 308), has two bar fragments which are almost certainly the two ends of an implement of this type. The missing middle section could have carried lugs.

Most of these bar-chisels are in Arreton Assemblage contexts and none is certainly earlier.

Axe-like ingots or 'blanks', *(Type series nos. 119-120)*
This is a difficult category to define or interpret. It originally derives from Harbison's recognition that within the prodigious Irish flat axe corpus there were some objects of rather amorphous form, potentially crudely shaped 'ingots' which nevertheless reflected an axe-like form (Harbison 1969, 22 – his inverted commas). His group is actually a miscellany; some objects are undoubtedly conventional types of axe in damaged or corroded state. In particular, axes of Sub-class 2D and hachettes of 2E are clearly recognisable, while some of the narrow examples probably belong to the axe-chisel family defined above.

A minority of the Irish examples exhibit clearly asymmetric profiles and are interpretable as blanks from a univalve mould; there are a couple of parallels in northern Britain (e.g. Tonderghie, Dumfries & Galloway – Britton 1963, 260 fig 2, 311) as well as occasional additional Irish examples classified amongst the axes – notably in the Glenalla hoard (Fig 15; Harbison 1969, nos 1582-1583; personal study).

Figure 15: One of two axe blanks in the Glenalla hoard, Co Donegal, associated with two 4E-like axes; scale 25%; drawing Stuart Needham

Setting aside potentially eroded axes and univalve blanks for axes, there are still a small number of rather amorphous objects – oval, sub-triangular, pear-shaped – of small size. They can also be rather thin, so little metal is present, and they may have unusual, non-lenticular profiles. Some of these at least do not appear to be badly eroded examples of finished axes; moreover, they are too small to have been destined for working up into standard sized axes. Without more detailed study, it is difficult to attribute a function, but they could have served an ingot function – that is, to facilitate the distribution of raw metal – as implied by Harbison's label. The alternative is that they too are blanks, but despite their vaguely axe-like shape, they were for other implements. The shape and size of some examples, such as that from Llancarfan Community (no 97) would have lent itself better to the production of flat daggers or knives and it is noteworthy that matrices for such objects occur on a few of the univalve stone moulds: Cambo, Northumberland; Foudland, Aberdeenshire; Culbin Sands, Morayshire; 'Suffolk Fens' (Britton 1963, 320-1, 323, fig 7, pl 26; Schmidt & Burgess 1981, nos. 296, 297, 301), and Lough Gall, Co Antrim (Collins 1970, 25, 26 fig 2).

Reflections and guidelines

At the time of completion of the original corpus in 1983, artefact studies and typological classification were at their lowest ebb in British Archaeology. This was not the sole reason for my failure to publish the forerunner of the scheme presented here, but it certainly contributed to its low prioritisation. That was a mistake, as becomes clearer year by year as new finds are reported to the Portable Antiquities Scheme. All the many relevant finds made since 1983 clamour for a framework in order to give them proper context. And in this advanced state of archaeology, in the early 21st century, such frameworks really *should* exist but frequently still do not. It is beholden on the discipline to create detailed and analytically rigorous typologies against which a range of other evidence can be compared. Creating a useful or meaningful typology is not a simple affair. Gathering together all the examples of a type and making a few superficial and unanalysed divisions is almost worthless, as is clear for example from Harbison's Irish corpus (even accepting that this was published almost half a century ago). Success in the endeavour, I would suggest, comes from deep familiarity with the material and from deep enquiry into the *process* and *context* of morphological change. Analytically rigorous the process must be, but intuitive thinking may also play a part.

The passage of years does of course offer a silver lining of sorts. In returning to the corpus anew it allowed almost fresh eyes to review decisions made leading up to 1983. Many stood the test of re-examination; a few did less well and revisions to the scheme have been made accordingly. Even where the original classification has remained unaltered, there can still sometimes be altered perception of relationships between the groups defined. We may often find consensus over morphological groupings made, yet hold different views on how they should be explained in relation to one another.

Classifying and interpreting the early metal age axes of southern Britain proved to be an enlightening experience in several ways. It showed for the first time just how many early axes there were from the region, even for relatively early stages of the sequence. Moreover, a high proportion of finds are from the eastern counties, well away from metalliferous zones. While numerically the corpus was still much inferior to that for Ireland, it was possible through careful and detailed analysis of form and decoration to argue a high degree of autonomy in the production of axes in the region, again from an early stage. This should not have been too surprising given the obvious insularity of contemporary British dagger styles and the fact that stone moulds for flat axes were known from Britain, including a few from the south, but such was the pervading assumption of an Irish origin for British finds of flat and low-flanged axes. This can now be laid to rest. It is probable that a rather small minority of axes are actual imports from Ireland despite Britain's heavy dependence on Irish copper during Period 1 and earlier Period 2, and despite the long-standing existence of allied style traditions amongst axes on the two sides of the Irish Sea. This broad-scale sharing of style traditions running through much of the sequence covered here finally dissolves in Period 4 as Class 5 axes in the two regions – Ireland and southern Britain – diverge more obviously in form and decoration. Dispelling the myth of a ubiquitous Irish origin also of course had implications for the finds of British-Irish axes (imitations as well as imports) on the Continent. Whenever origin is ambiguous on morphological grounds, the weight of probability must now shift to origins in Britain simply due to its much greater proximity to northern Europe, whence most of the relevant finds have come. As an aside here, the desperate need for a more detailed and accurate classification of Irish Chalcolithic and Early Bronze Age axes has been a recurrent theme running through the above text.

Another common misconception, perhaps, is that flat and low-flanged axes are simple forms. At a certain technological level this may be true, but what is astonishing about the insular axe series is the sheer diversity of shapes and profiles represented through the sequence, and upon this is laid a rich repertoire of decoration. It represents a constant stream of creativity on the part of the metalworkers responsible for axe production. There is further significance to be drawn regarding the way change takes place. Notwithstanding occasional minor disjunctures in the sequence (see further below), the overall picture is one of perpetual development – or 'evolution'. In recent decades, 'evolution' has become a by-word for all that was wrong with typologies and classification. Yet the problem was often misdiagnosed. Typological ordering based *solely* on 'logical' typological connections was a fitting target for criticism. It was the assumption of a single 'logical' progression that was flawed, not the creation of typologies *per se*. In the case of Chalcolithic and Early Bronze Age axes we have increasing patterning in associations, a few directly associated radiocarbon dates and also changing patterns in metal composition and decoration, all serving as checks on the validity of a typological sequence. Collectively they give tremendous support to the interpreted sequence and the nuances of development that may be discerned (Fig 16).

The evolution of early metal age axes is rarely unilinear, a deduction echoed in the recent assessments of contemporary halberd and dagger development (Needham et al. 2015; Needham et al. 2017). Instead it is possible to trace multiple pathways of development (Fig 16). In suggesting that the pattern was one of continuous development, it should not be supposed that it took place at a constant rate. There were undoubtedly periodic bursts of change and longer periods of relative stasis, but arguing rate changes in detail is inhibited by likely oscillations in rates of deposition. A hypothetical example of the effects of a failing metal supply on permanent deposition rates has been advanced elsewhere (Needham 2007, 283). Such a scenario could, for example, mean that the strong statistical separation of Class 4 and 5 axes was in reality less marked and consequently the evolution of the latter class more gradual than is apparent. Regardless of whether a lull in deposition occurred at this particular juncture, it is nevertheless clear that evolution was at play across this divide, for there is no wholesale change in morphology; the disjuncture, if it is real, lies in one single attribute – flange height. The same is true at a much earlier horizon, that straddling the metallurgical transition of copper to bronze. Axes may suddenly have been furnished with narrower butts than before, but there is a good stylistic comparison in all other respects (Fig 16: 2C→3A and 2D→3C). To argue that this too is part of an evolutionary trajectory does not undermine the potential social significance attached to the decision to make bronze axes with consistently narrower butts than their copper equivalents (Needham 2004), but it does illustrate the potential importance of quite nuanced changes in morphology.

Overall then, early metal age axes are viewed by the writer as forming a fairly seamless topography of interactions and style gradations. Some transects across this topography are gentle undulations, others encounter ridges, crags or ravines, and yet others may cross entirely featureless terrain in which change is minimal and gradual, but all ultimately interconnects with all. In more conventional, statistical terms the 'topography' comprises two possible elements: a series of nodes, each having apparent significance through the repetition of correlating attributes, yet each grading in certain directions towards other nodes; and a more uniform 'plain' formed of a polythetic set of attribute associations with little by way of specific repeating patterns. Our job in classifying objects in this 'topography of form' is to hope, firstly, to identify the nodes and bound them as meaningfully as possible. Second and equally important is to divide the planar material into useful groups. Just because there are no landmarks, or nodes, it does not mean there are no meaningful changes from one side of the plain to the other; conditions will have changed gradationally and the next nearest landscapes in various directions may be entirely different in character from one another. Translated into object classification terminology, that difference in character may be temporal, geographical or social, and it is the standard archaeological method of comparing typologies against other branches of evidence that allows one to draw useful boundaries across the flatter morphological landscapes. If we want to draw the maximum information from such material, then we must attempt to draw those boundaries.

Drawing boundaries, however, must be done systematically otherwise it is in danger of being misleading about formal relationships and their wider significance. In this advanced state of archaeological methodologies it really is not good enough to rely on informal evaluation by every observer independently according to their own sense of objectivity. The application of the current classification scheme to new finds may not be immediate or easy, but it does offer reliability and genuine inter-comparability. With advances in shape recognition using digital methods, there must be the prospect of at least partially automating this procedure in the near future.

Before attempting the classification of a new find, it must first be assessed for its *surface condition*. Recognition of when an axe has been surface reduced is crucial for any object whose classification may rely on the presence or absence of quite subtle features or on finely drawn metrical boundaries. Moreover, surface condition, as it becomes worse, may obscure evidence for breaks causing uncertainty over the object's degree of completeness. Amongst the classic signs of surface deterioration and reduction are: rounded-off body angles, irregularities along the top of flanges, frequent surface pitting or pocking, undulating surfaces and 'dusty' surfaces. Irregularities in thin edges that are not easily explained as resulting from chipping or blunting are likely often to be due to localised variations in the thickness of corrosion and consequent flaking. Differences only need to be small alongside thinning edges for there to be a disproportionate effect on the original outline, hence leading to waviness. Occasionally axes retain a split-level surface, the prouder level representing the original (but oxidised) surface with potential for subtle evidence of working and fine decoration, the lower level instead being stripped and lacking in such detail. The two levels can be separated by less than a millimetre.

Having evaluated surface condition, the next stage is to assess completeness condition. Major fractures are usually obvious, but where there is the possibility of a minor portion broken off, it may not be easy to decide if surface reduction has rounded off the crisp angles of fracture. Nor would it be easy to determine whether there had been any reworking of the damaged area to 'renew' the object. These things can be readily seen on axes in good condition, but are a matter for conjecture on less well preserved ones. The consequences for attribution to a classification scheme based on metrical values are major; for example, the unrecognised loss of even a small butt end of an axe could take its metrical ratios well away from its original value and falsely place the object in another sub-class. An example from the Willerby hoard was discussed above; it is only the fact that its condition is good that allows it to be seen that the haft-end is over-short and for it to be posited that this was due to miscasting or fracture with subsequent reworking.

It needs to be recognised then that some axes are inherently less capable of full or confident classification and the answer to this is to accept wholeheartedly that an object should only be classified to a level that is consonant with its condition. This is where a hierarchical classification system pays dividends. The great majority of complete or near-complete axes can be attributed with some confidence to one of the principal classes, 1-5, and many can be taken further if the original outline survives or can be reconstructed with some confidence. However, firm classification to sub-class or type level demands careful evaluation, measurement and calculation. Where this is not done, it is suggested that attribution should be more tentative and expressed as: *Class X (cf Sub-class Y)*. This appellation is also appropriate whenever condition is too poor for confident attribution. Table 4 summarises the level to which classification should be taken in different circumstances. This can only be a guide, since every situation is different, but it does highlight the complex interplay between surface condition, completeness condition and the level of classification possible. The principles here are more widely applicable to copper and bronze metalwork, although the detail may need to be adjusted for other broad categories of object. Where form is intrinsically more complex, as for example for palstaves, there will be less uncertainty over degree of completeness as surface condition worsens.

Finally, it may also be helpful to offer a *critical path* for the classification of early metal age axes and related objects (those in reasonably good surface and completeness conditions) and this is provided in Appendix 2.

Acknowledgements
Research such as involved here relies on the provision of facilities by museums and much support from their curatorial staff; to these and private owners of relevant material, my sincere thanks. Specific help in drawing up this paper has come from Adam Gwilt, Neil Wilkin, Brendan O'Connor and Matt Knight.

Table 4: Suggested levels of classification according to condition of object and degree of study

Surface condition	Completeness condition	Informal assessment	Full metrical analysis
Excellent to good – very little if any surface loss	Complete	To Class (*cf* Sub-class)	To Class, Sub-class and Type
	Little missing – original outlines reconstruct-able with confidence	To Class (*cf* Sub-class)	To Class, Sub-class and Type
	Significant portion (but still less than half) missing – only approximate reconstruction possible	To Class (possibly *cf* Sub-class)	
	Only a fragment of blade or haft end represented	To *cf* Class [at best]	
Incomplete survival of original surface	Complete	To Class (*cf* Sub-class)	To Class, Sub-class and possibly Type
	Little missing – original outlines reconstruct-able with fair confidence	To Class (*cf* Sub-class)	To Class, Sub-class and possibly Type
	Significant portion (but still less than half) missing – only approximate reconstruction possible	To Class (possibly *cf* Sub-class)	
	Only a fragment of blade or haft end represented	To *cf* Class [at best]	
Minor survival of original surface	Complete – original outlines predictable to some degree	Probably to Class	To Class (*cf* Sub-class)
	Relatively little missing, but original outlines rather uncertain	Probably to Class	To Class (*cf* Sub-class)
	Significant portion missing (still less than half)	Possibly to Class	
	Only a fragment of blade or haft end represented	To *cf* Class [at best]	
Surface totally reduced, but general morphology seemingly retained	Seemingly complete – original outlines only approximately reconstruct-able	Possibly to Class	Probably to Class (possibly *cf* Sub-class)
	Seemingly little missing – original outlines only approximately reconstruct-able	Possibly to Class	Probably to Class (possibly *cf* Sub-class)
	Probably significant portion missing	Possibly to Class	
	Only a fragment of blade or haft end represented	Possibly to early metal age axe [at best]	
Amorphous due to extensive corrosion loss	Seemingly complete or little loss	Probably to early metal age axe [at best]	
	Uncertain how much of object represented	Possibly to early metal age axe	
	Probably only a minor fragment represented	Possibly to early metal age axe [at best]	

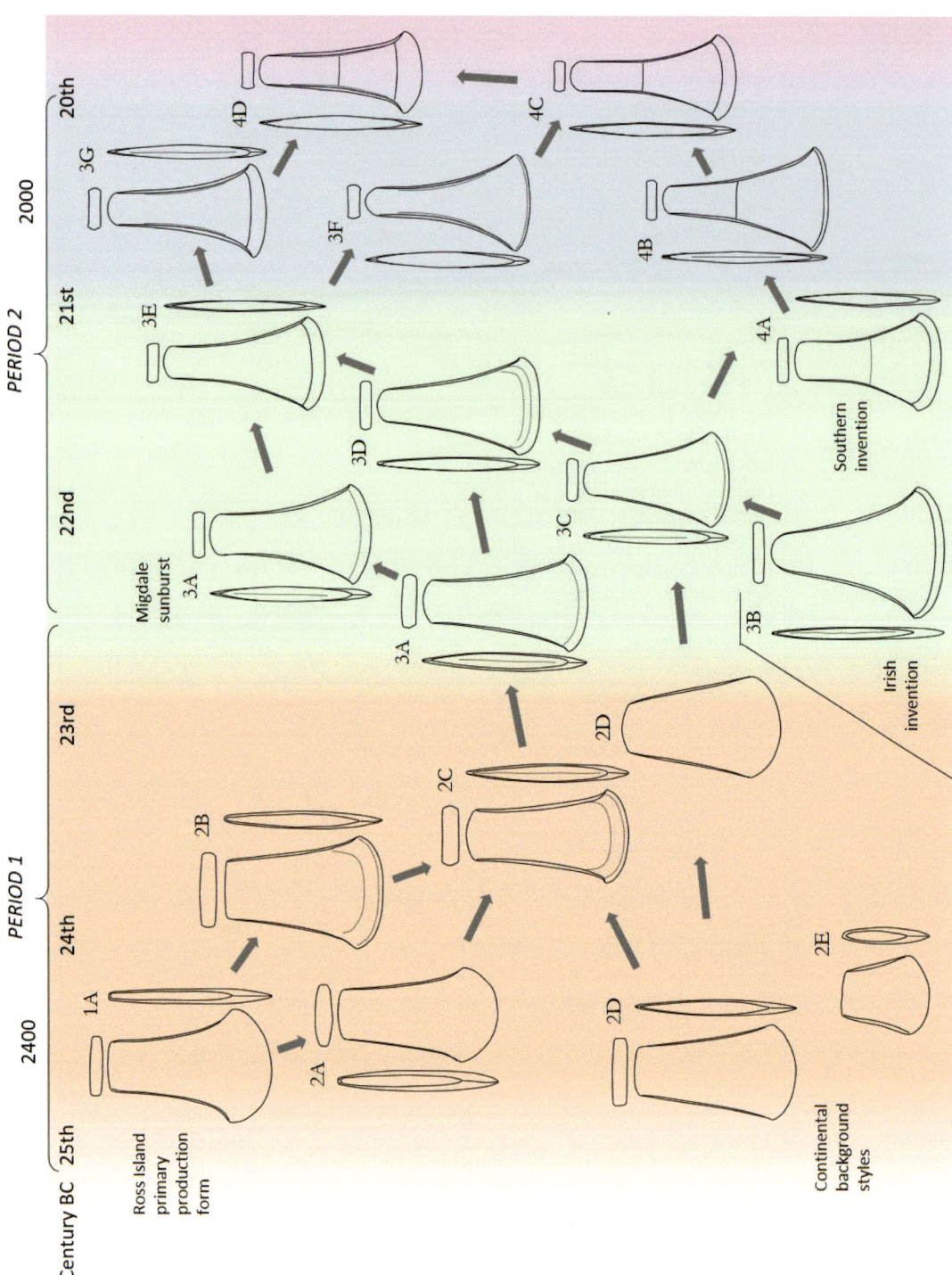

Figure 16: Typological threads in the evolution of axes during the Chalcolithic and Early Bronze Age in southern Britain; drawing: Stuart Needham

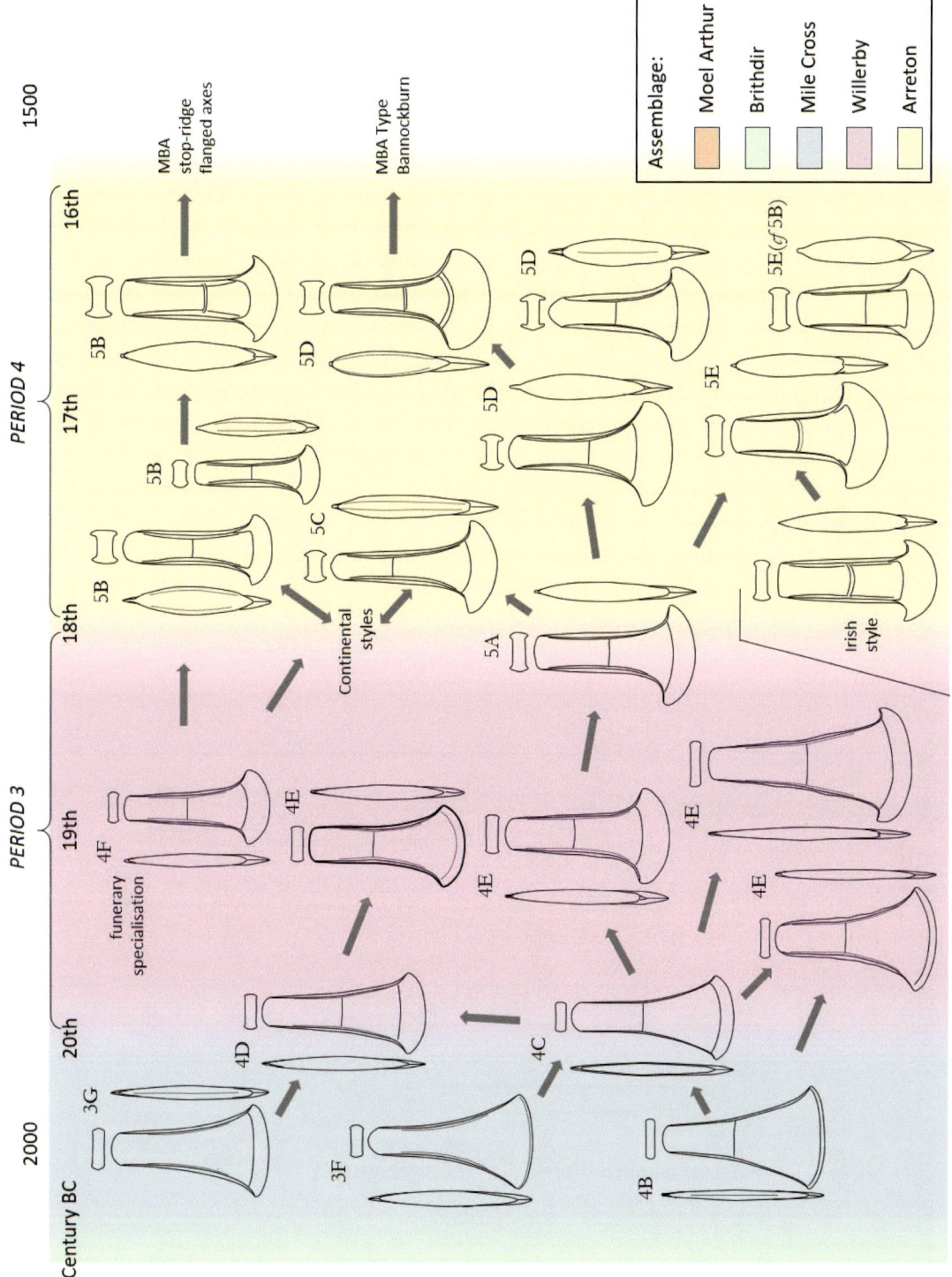

Figure 16 (continued): Typological threads in the evolution of axes during the Chalcolithic and Early Bronze Age in southern Britain; drawing: Stuart Needham

Type series of Chalcolithic & Early Bronze Age axe-heads for southern Britain

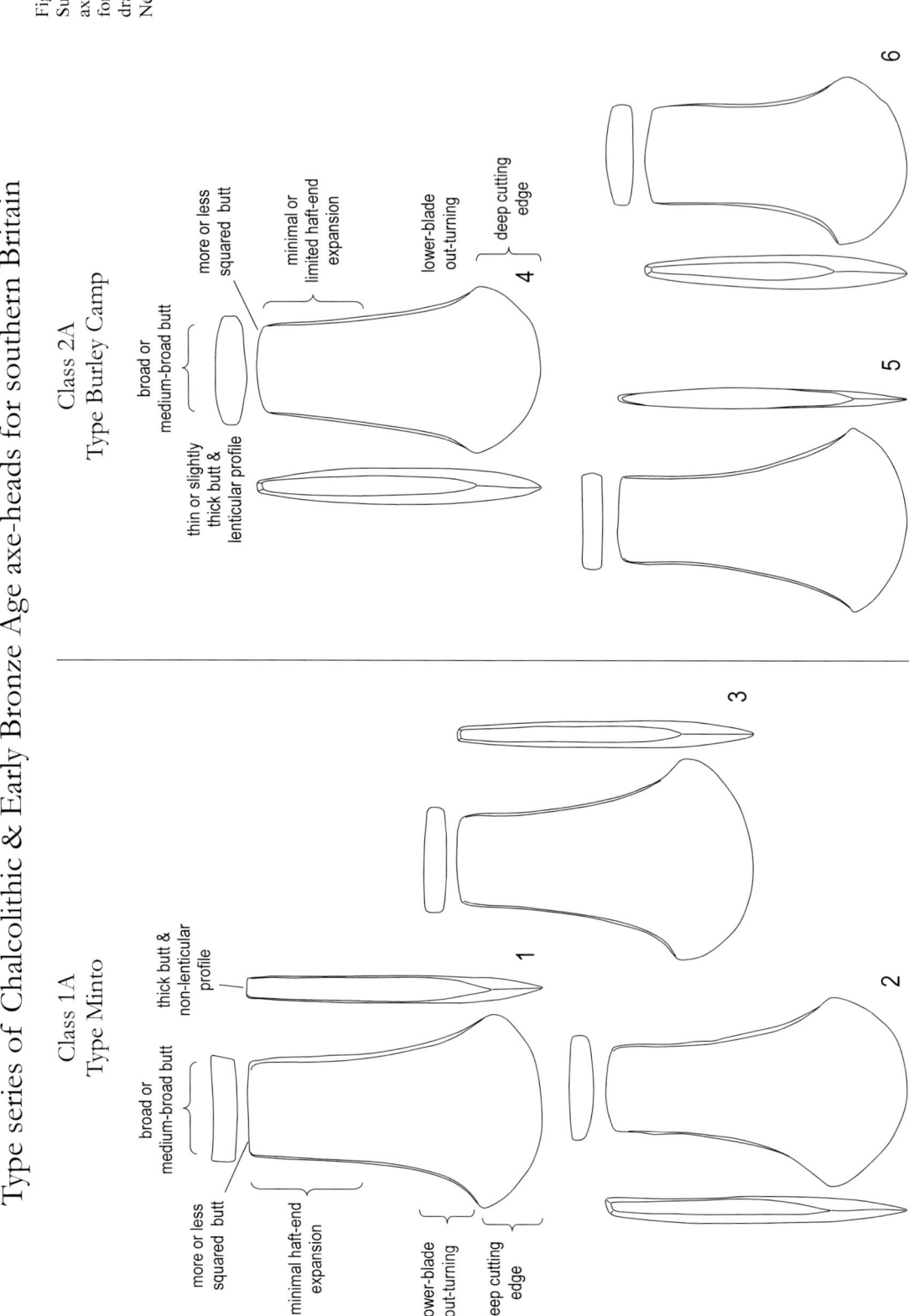

Figure 17: Examples of Sub-class 1A and 2A axes; see Appendix 1 for objects represented; drawings Stuart Needham

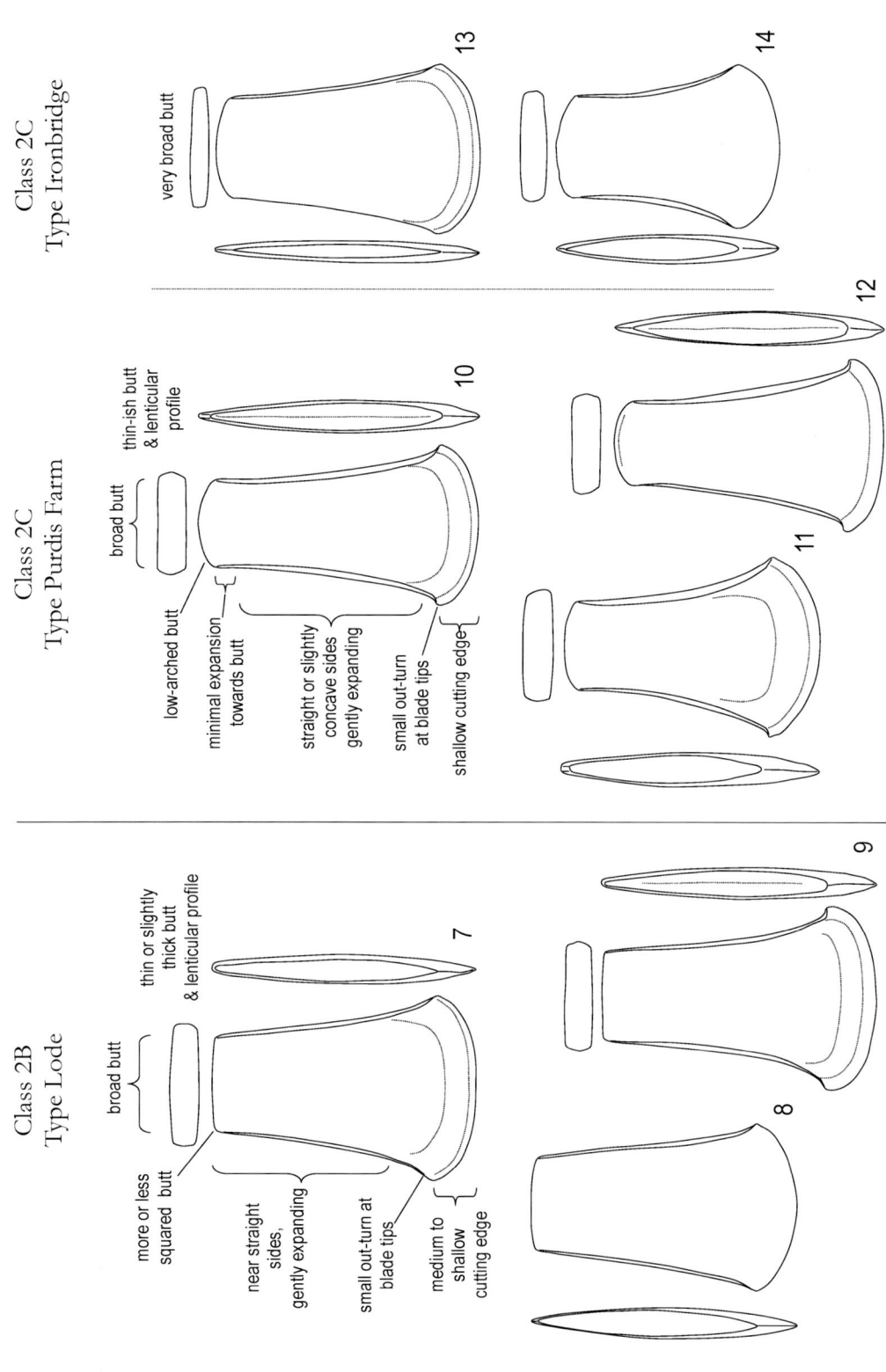

Figure 18: Examples of Sub-class 2B and 2C axes; see Appendix 1 for objects represented; drawings Stuart Needham

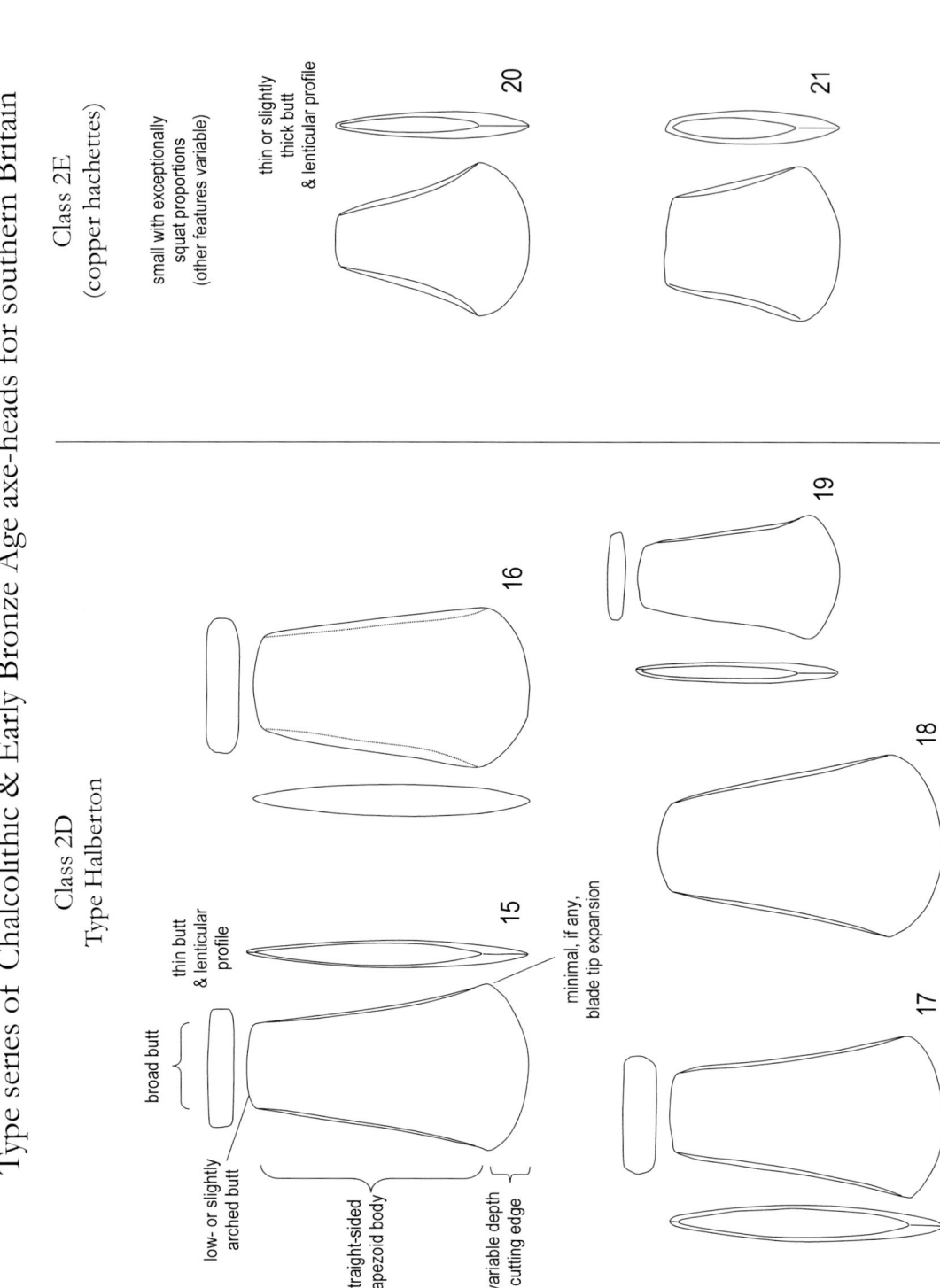

Figure 19: Examples of Sub-class 2D and 2E axes; see Appendix 1 for objects represented; drawings Stuart Needham

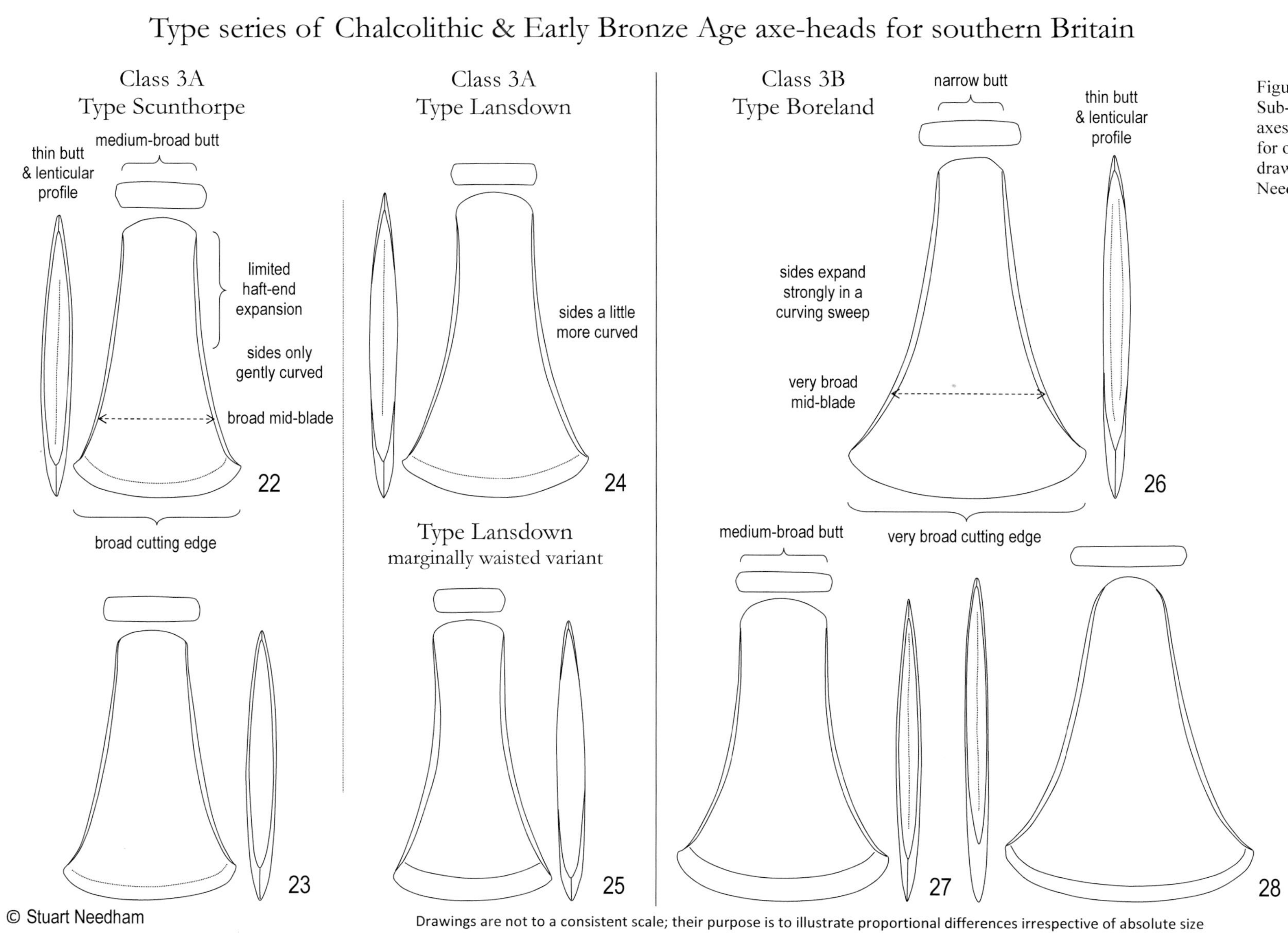

Type series of Chalcolithic & Early Bronze Age axe-heads for southern Britain

Class 3A
Type Scunthorpe

Class 3A
Type Lansdown

Class 3B
Type Boreland

Figure 20: Examples of Sub-class 3A and 3B axes; see Appendix 1 for objects represented; drawings Stuart Needham

medium-broad butt

limited haft-end expansion

sides only gently curved

broad mid-blade

broad cutting edge

thin butt & lenticular profile

sides a little more curved

Type Lansdown marginally waisted variant

narrow butt

sides expand strongly in a curving sweep

very broad mid-blade

very broad cutting edge

thin butt & lenticular profile

medium-broad butt

22
23
24
25
26
27
28

© Stuart Needham

Drawings are not to a consistent scale; their purpose is to illustrate proportional differences irrespective of absolute size

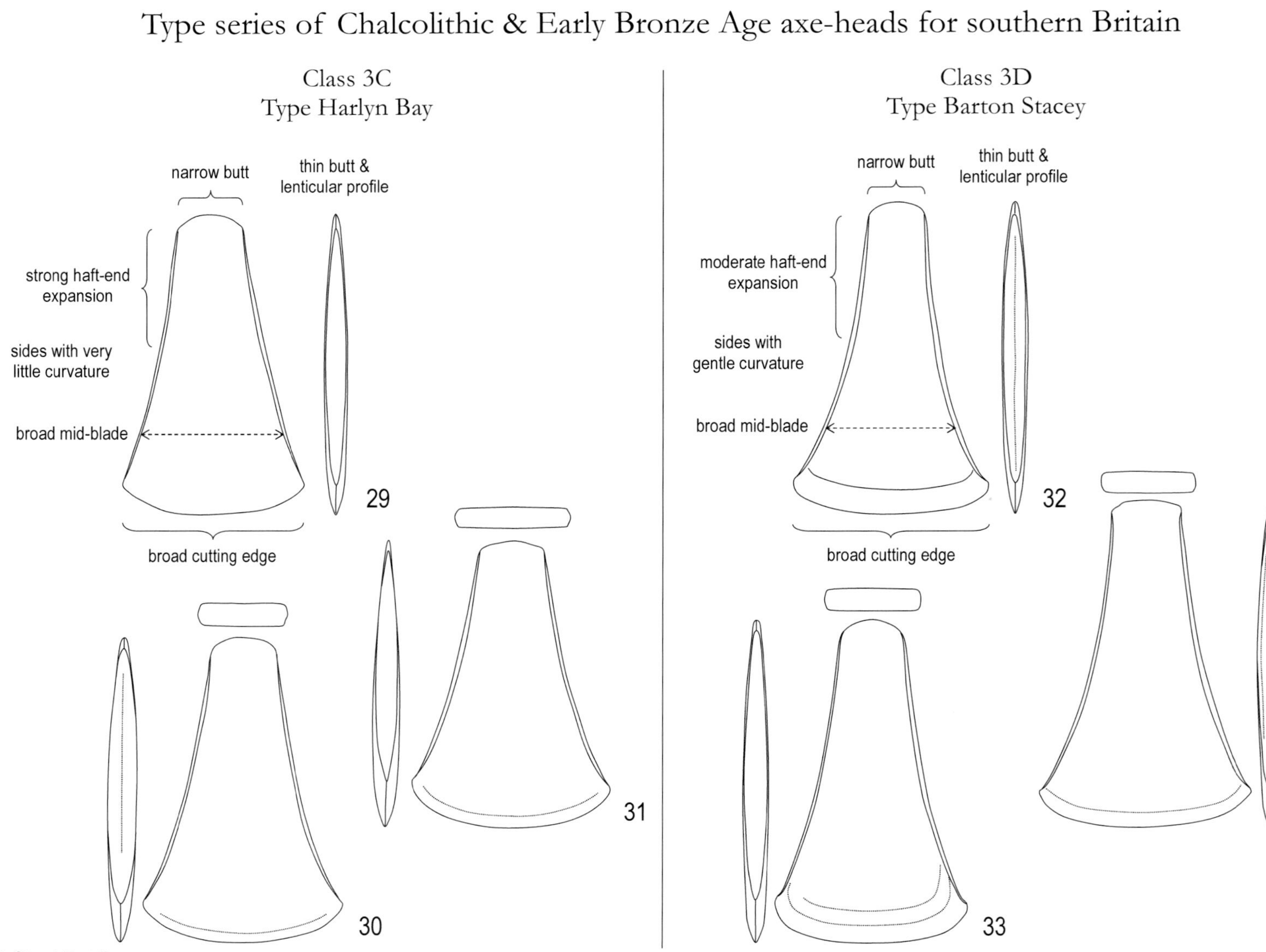

Type series of Chalcolithic & Early Bronze Age axe-heads for southern Britain

Class 3C
Type Harlyn Bay

thin butt & lenticular profile

narrow butt

strong haft-end expansion

sides with very little curvature

broad mid-blade

broad cutting edge

29

30

31

Class 3D
Type Barton Stacey

thin butt & lenticular profile

narrow butt

moderate haft-end expansion

sides with gentle curvature

broad mid-blade

broad cutting edge

32

33

34

Figure 21: Examples of Sub-class 3C and 3D axes; see Appendix 1 for objects represented; drawings Stuart Needham

Drawings are not to a consistent scale; their purpose is to illustrate proportional differences irrespective of absolute size

© Stuart Needham

Type series of Chalcolithic & Early Bronze Age axe-heads for southern Britain

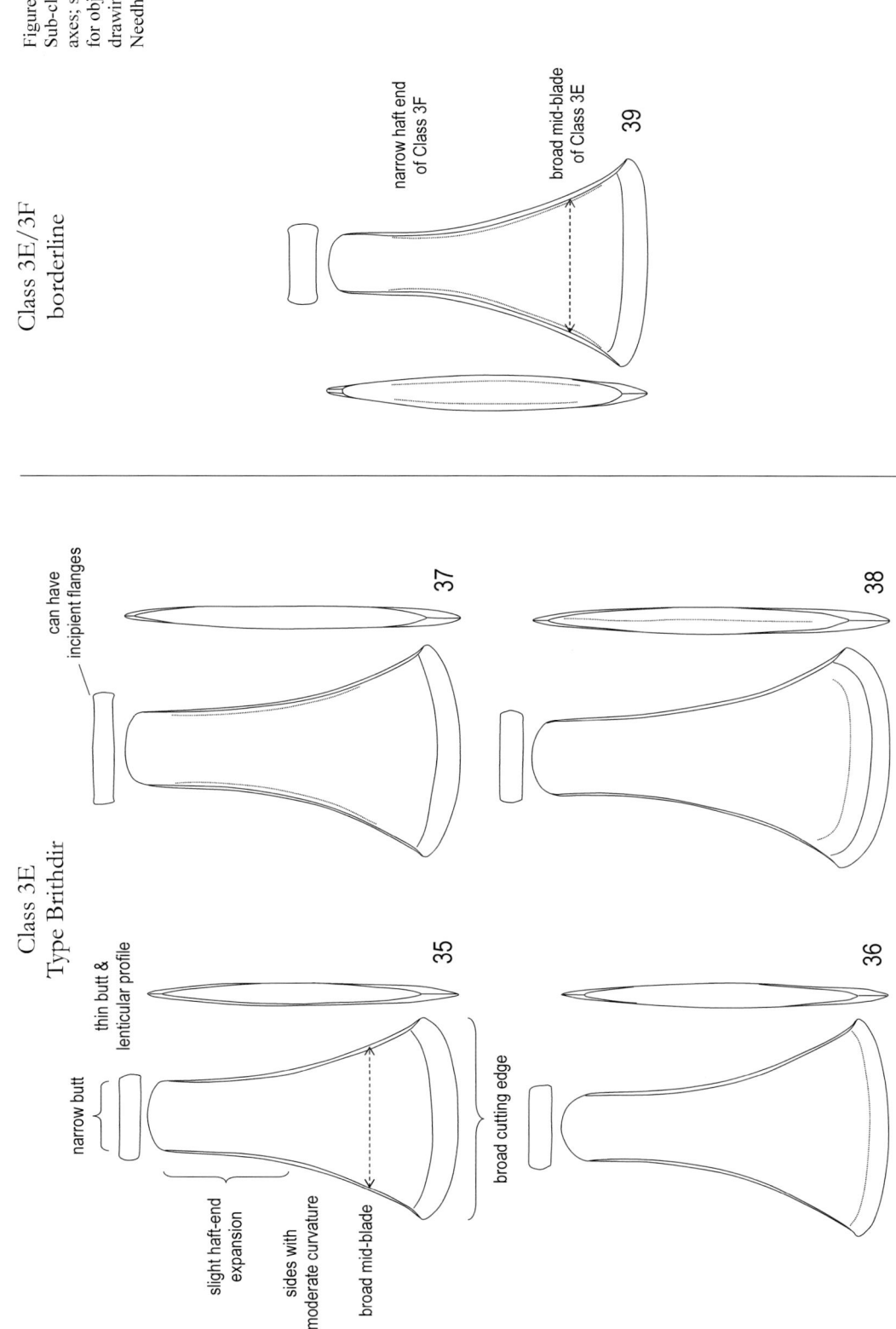

Figure 22: Examples of Sub-class 3E and 3E/3F axes; see Appendix 1 for objects represented; drawings Stuart Needham

Drawings are not to a consistent scale; their purpose is to illustrate proportional differences irrespective of absolute size

© Stuart Needham

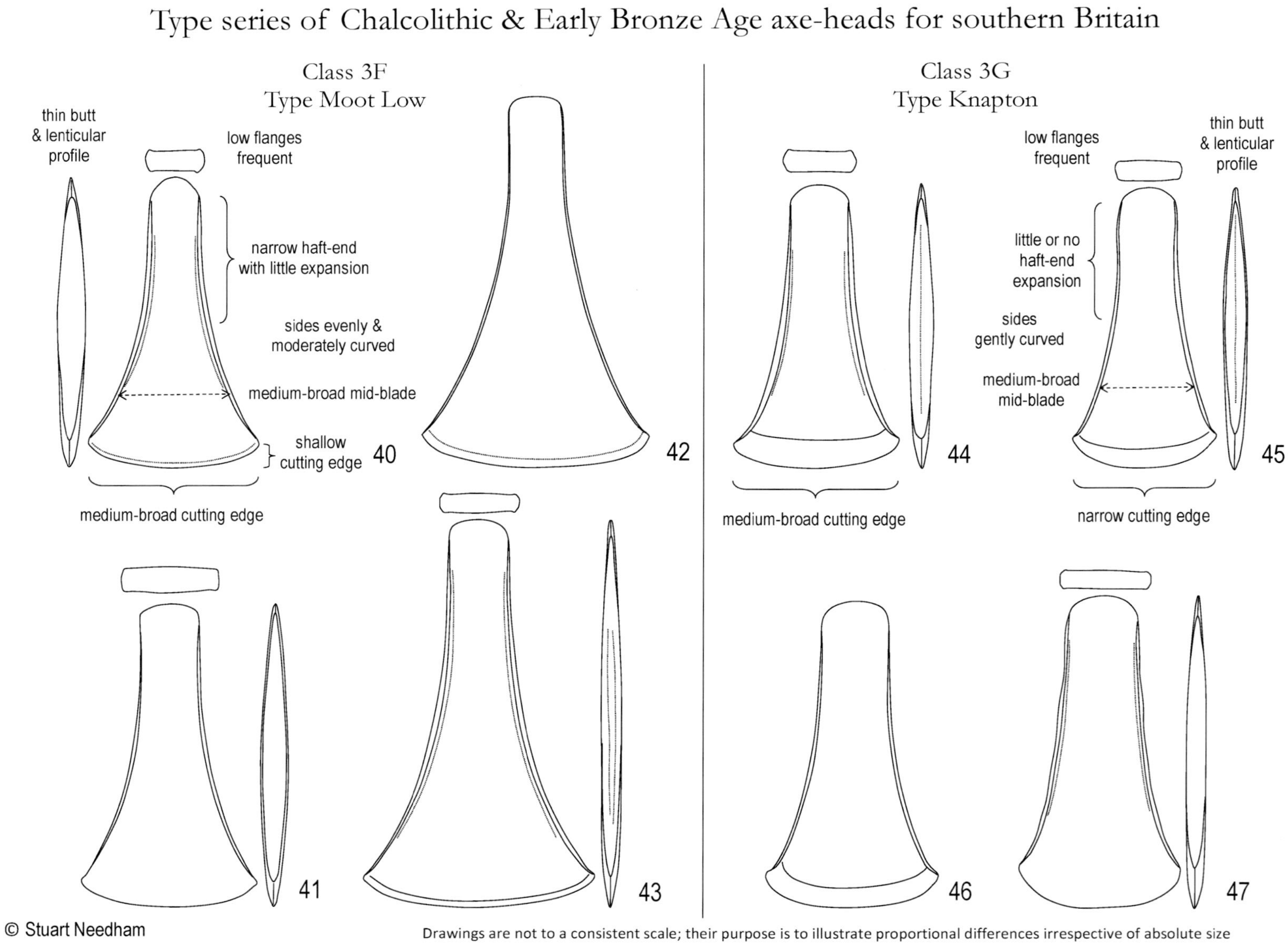

Type series of Chalcolithic & Early Bronze Age axe-heads for southern Britain

Class 3F
Type Moot Low

- low flanges frequent
- thin butt & lenticular profile
- narrow haft-end with little expansion
- sides evenly & moderately curved
- medium-broad mid-blade
- shallow cutting edge
- medium-broad cutting edge

40

41

42

43

Class 3G
Type Knapton

- low flanges frequent
- thin butt & lenticular profile
- little or no haft-end expansion
- sides gently curved
- medium-broad mid-blade
- medium-broad cutting edge
- narrow cutting edge

44

45

46

47

Figure 23: Examples of Sub-class 3F and 3G axes; see Appendix 1 for objects represented; drawings Stuart Needham

Drawings are not to a consistent scale; their purpose is to illustrate proportional differences irrespective of absolute size

© Stuart Needham

Type series of Chalcolithic & Early Bronze Age axe-heads for southern Britain

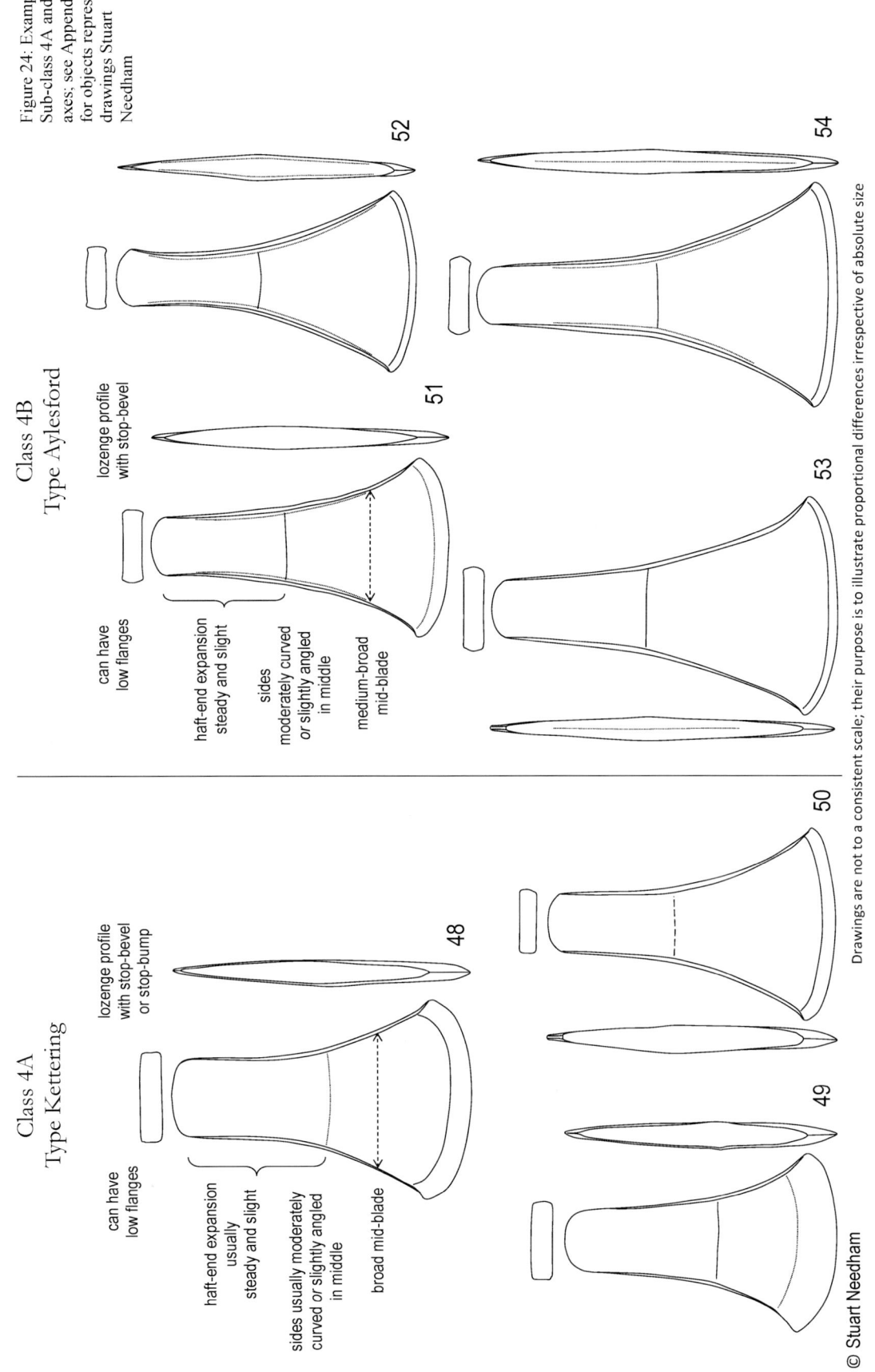

Figure 24: Examples of Sub-class 4A and 4B axes; see Appendix 1 for objects represented; drawings Stuart Needham

Type series of Chalcolithic & Early Bronze Age axe-heads for southern Britain

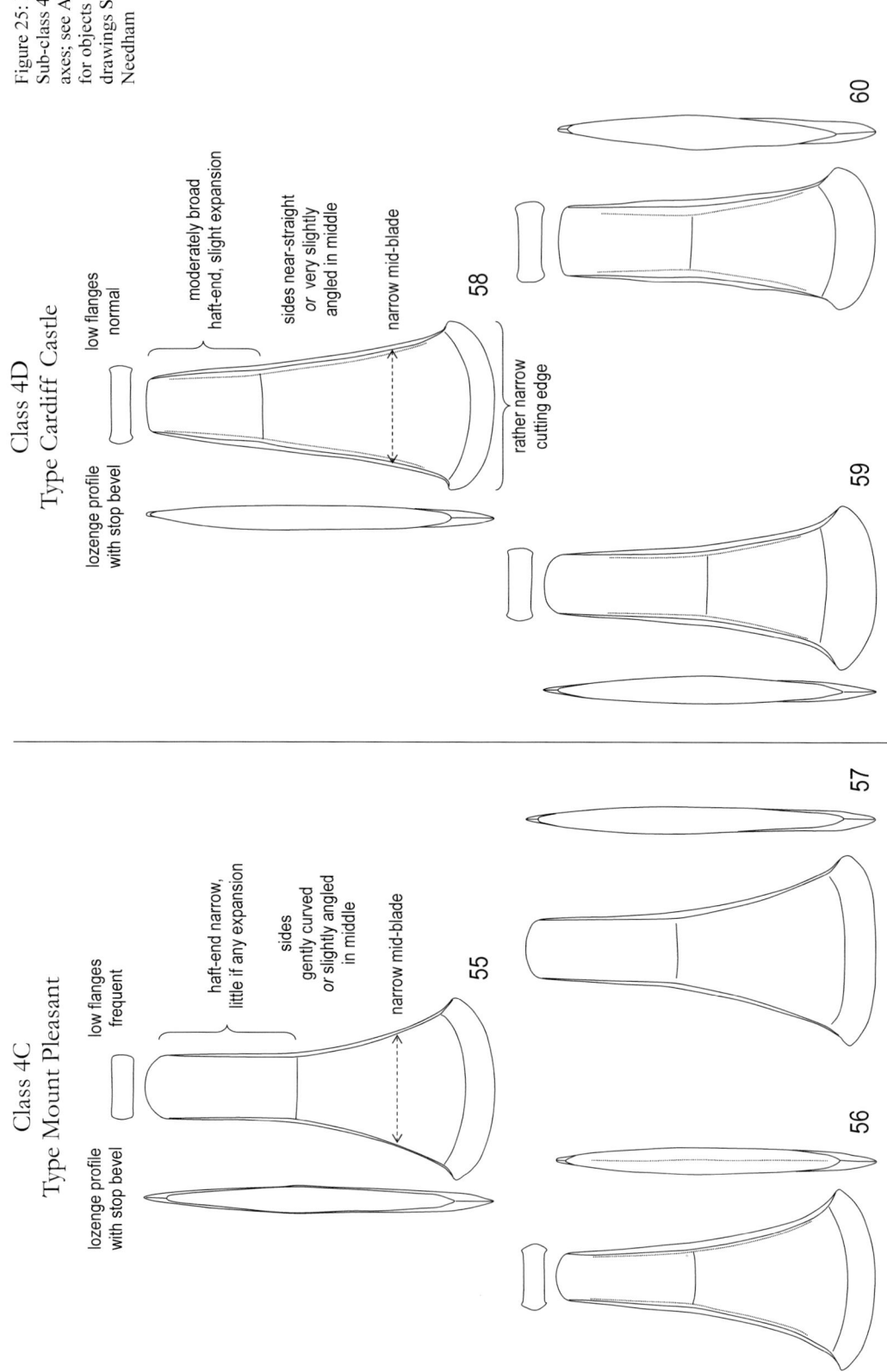

Figure 25: Examples of Sub-class 4C and 4D axes; see Appendix 1 for objects represented; drawings Stuart Needham

Drawings are not to a consistent scale; their purpose is to illustrate proportional differences irrespective of absolute size

© Stuart Needham

Type series of Chalcolithic & Early Bronze Age axe-heads for southern Britain

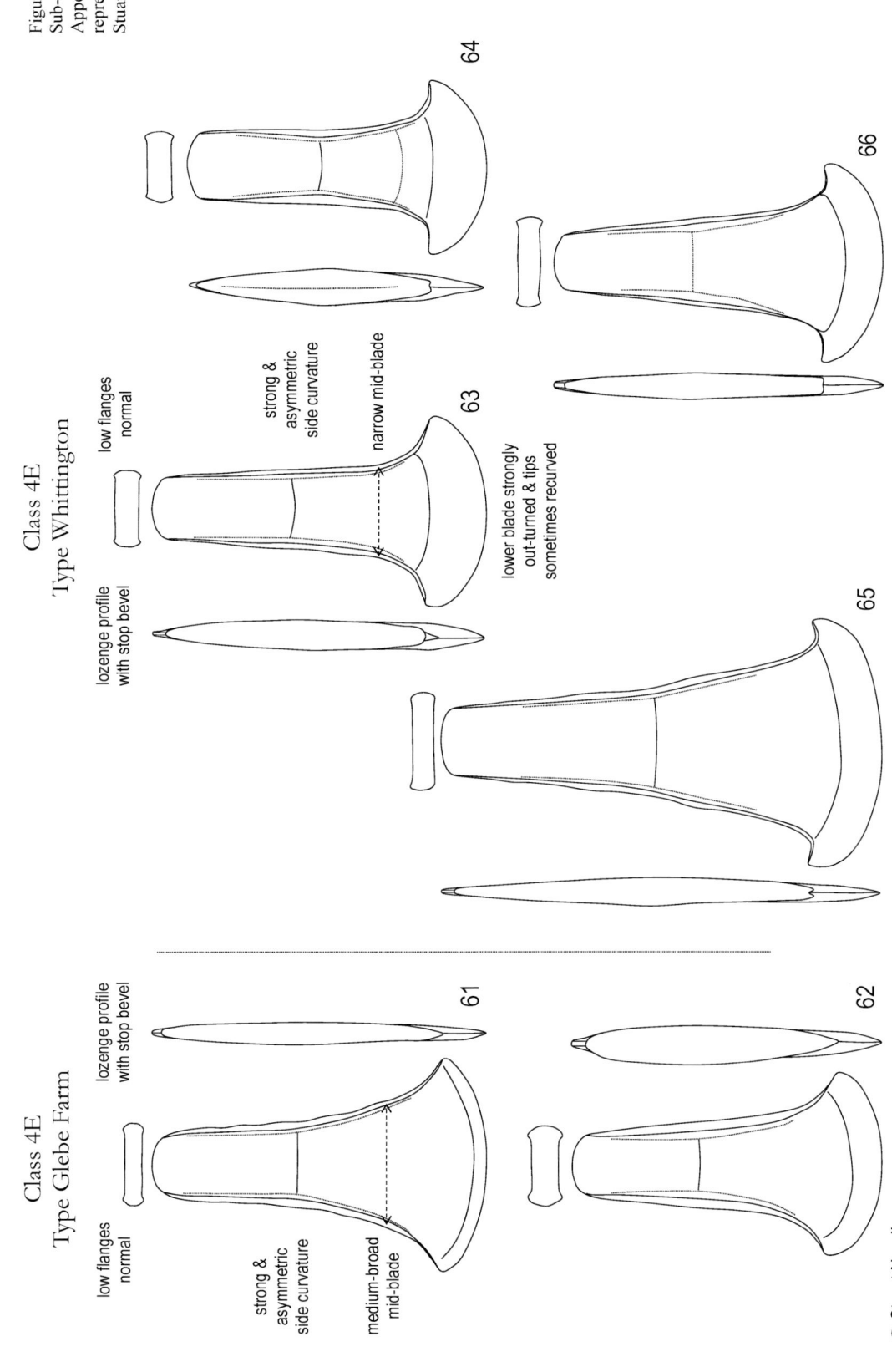

Figure 26: Examples of Sub-class 4E axes; see Appendix 1 for objects represented; drawings Stuart Needham

Type series of Chalcolithic & Early Bronze Age axe-heads for southern Britain

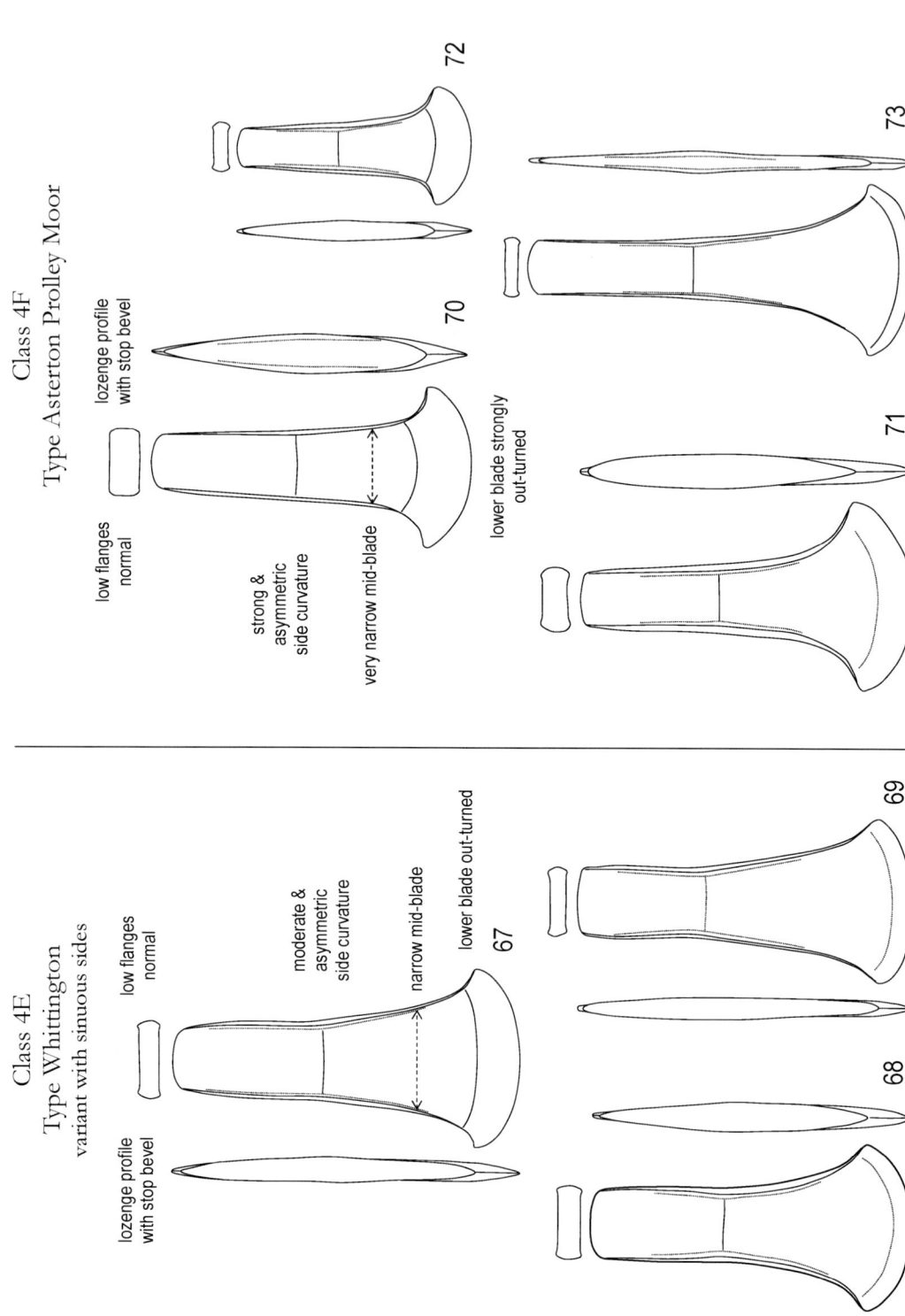

Figure 27: Examples of Sub-class 4E and 4F axes; see Appendix 1 for objects represented; drawings Stuart Needham

Type series of Chalcolithic & Early Bronze Age axe-heads for southern Britain

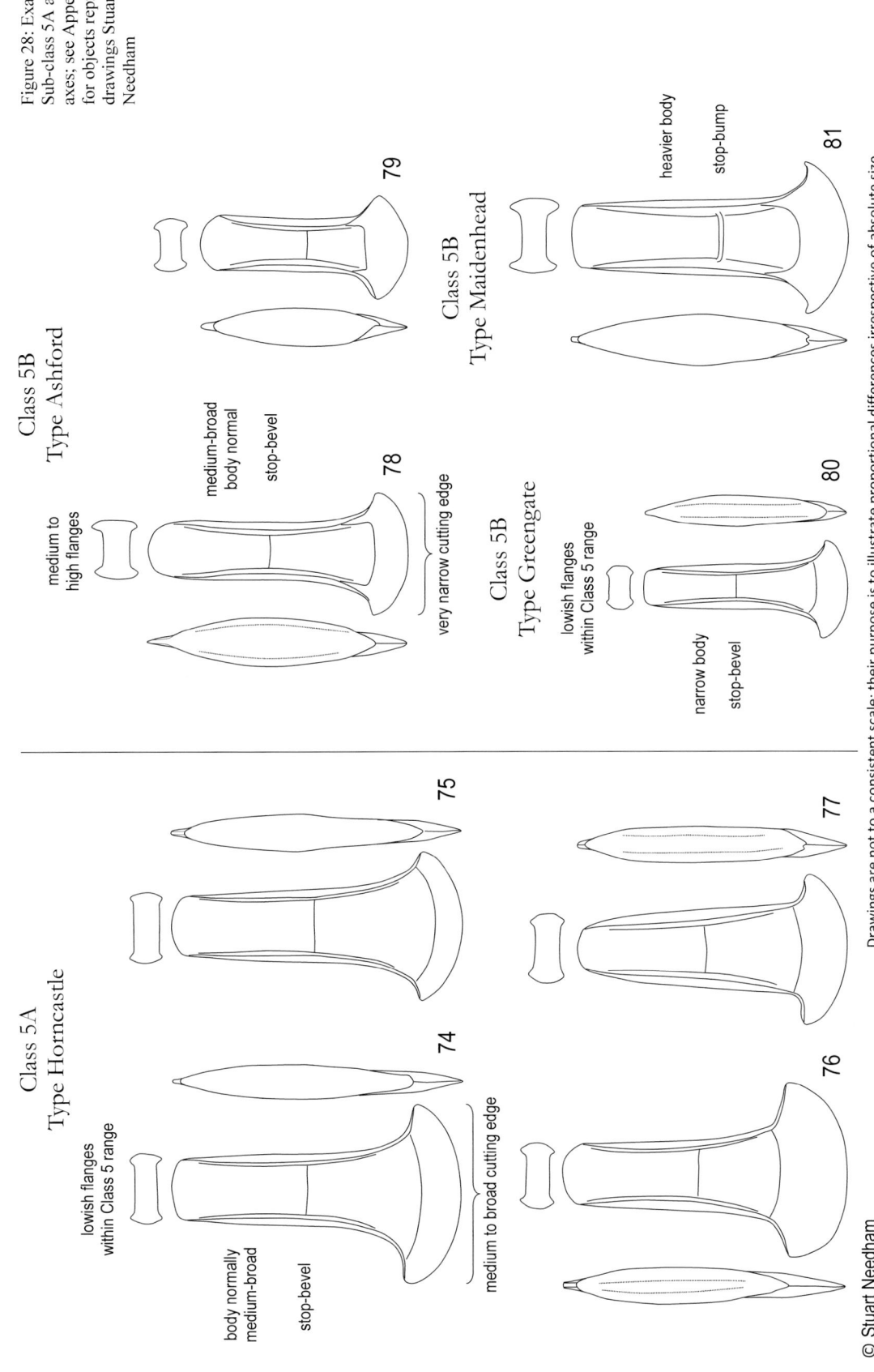

Figure 28: Examples of Sub-class 5A and 5B axes; see Appendix 1 for objects represented; drawings Stuart Needham

Drawings are not to a consistent scale; their purpose is to illustrate proportional differences irrespective of absolute size.

© Stuart Needham

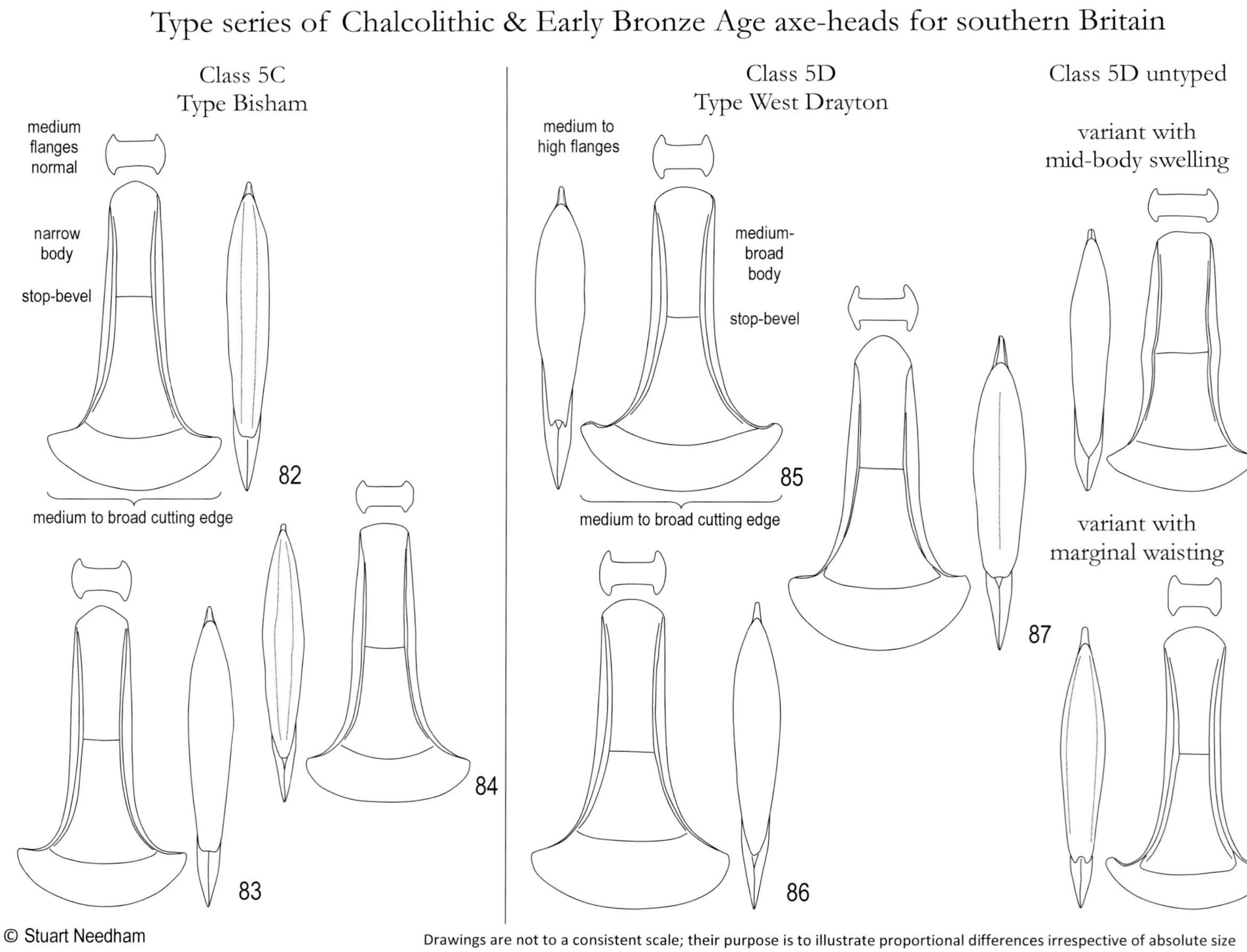

Type series of Chalcolithic & Early Bronze Age axe-heads for southern Britain

Class 5C
Type Bisham

medium flanges normal

narrow body

stop-bevel

medium to broad cutting edge

82

83

84

Class 5D
Type West Drayton

medium to high flanges

medium-broad body

stop-bevel

medium to broad cutting edge

85

86

87

Class 5D untyped

variant with mid-body swelling

88

variant with marginal waisting

89

Figure 29: Examples of Sub-class 5C and 5D axes; see Appendix 1 for objects represented; drawings Stuart Needham

Drawings are not to a consistent scale; their purpose is to illustrate proportional differences irrespective of absolute size

© Stuart Needham

Type series of Chalcolithic & Early Bronze Age axe-heads for southern Britain

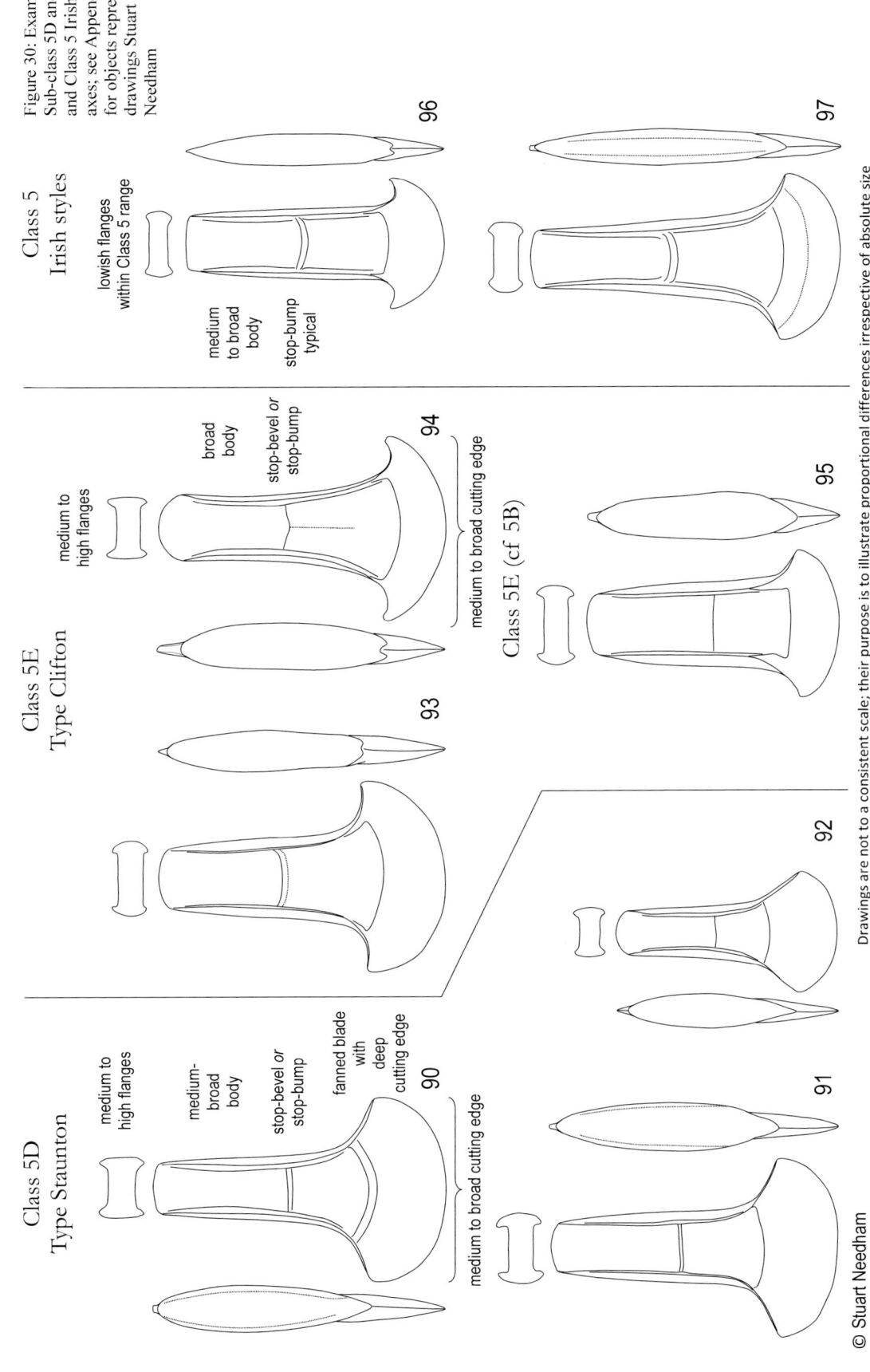

Figure 30: Examples of Sub-class 5D and 5E and Class 5 Irish styles axes; see Appendix 1 for objects represented; drawings Stuart Needham

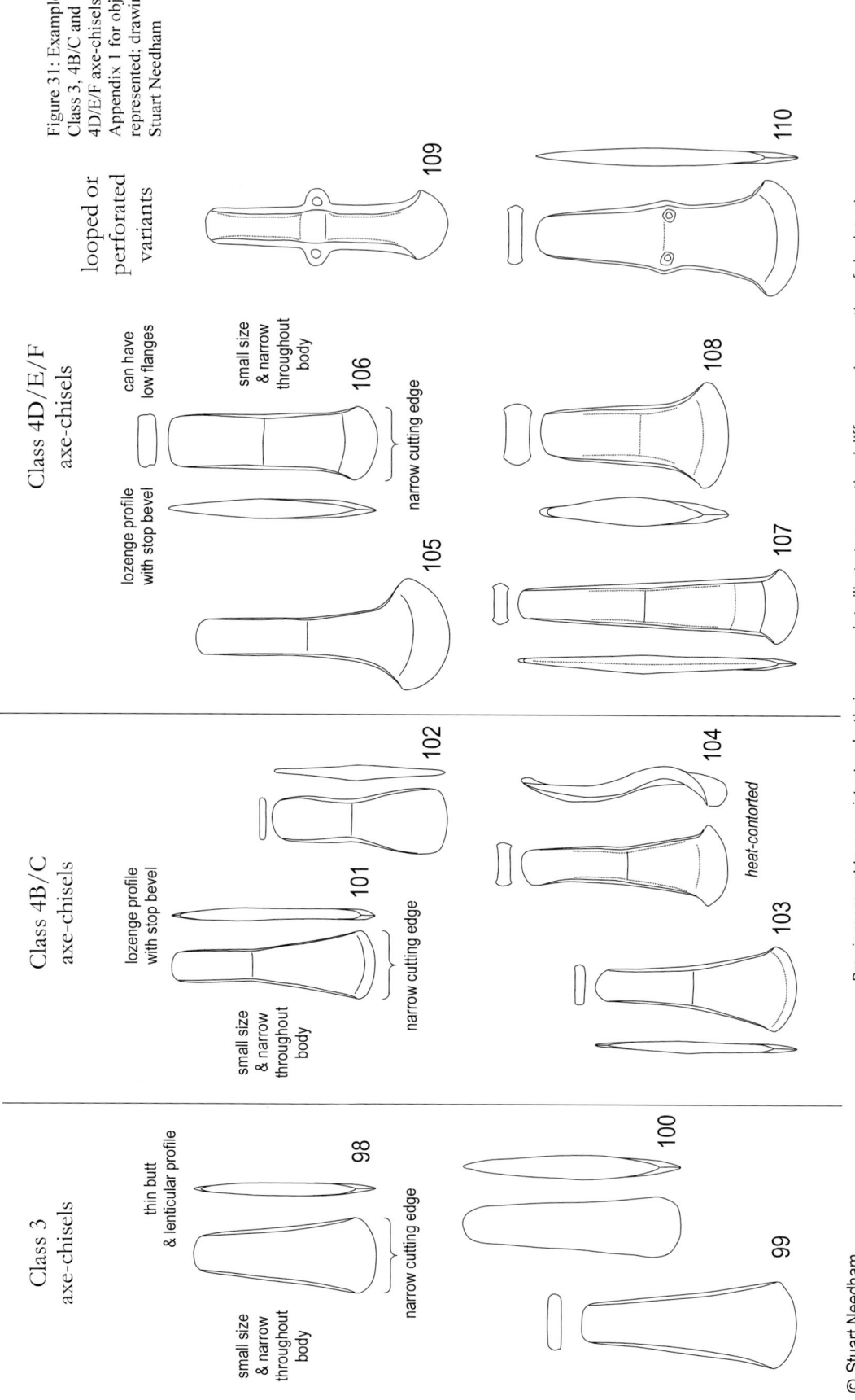

Figure 31: Examples of Class 3, 4B/C and 4D/E/F axe-chisels; see Appendix 1 for objects represented; drawings Stuart Needham

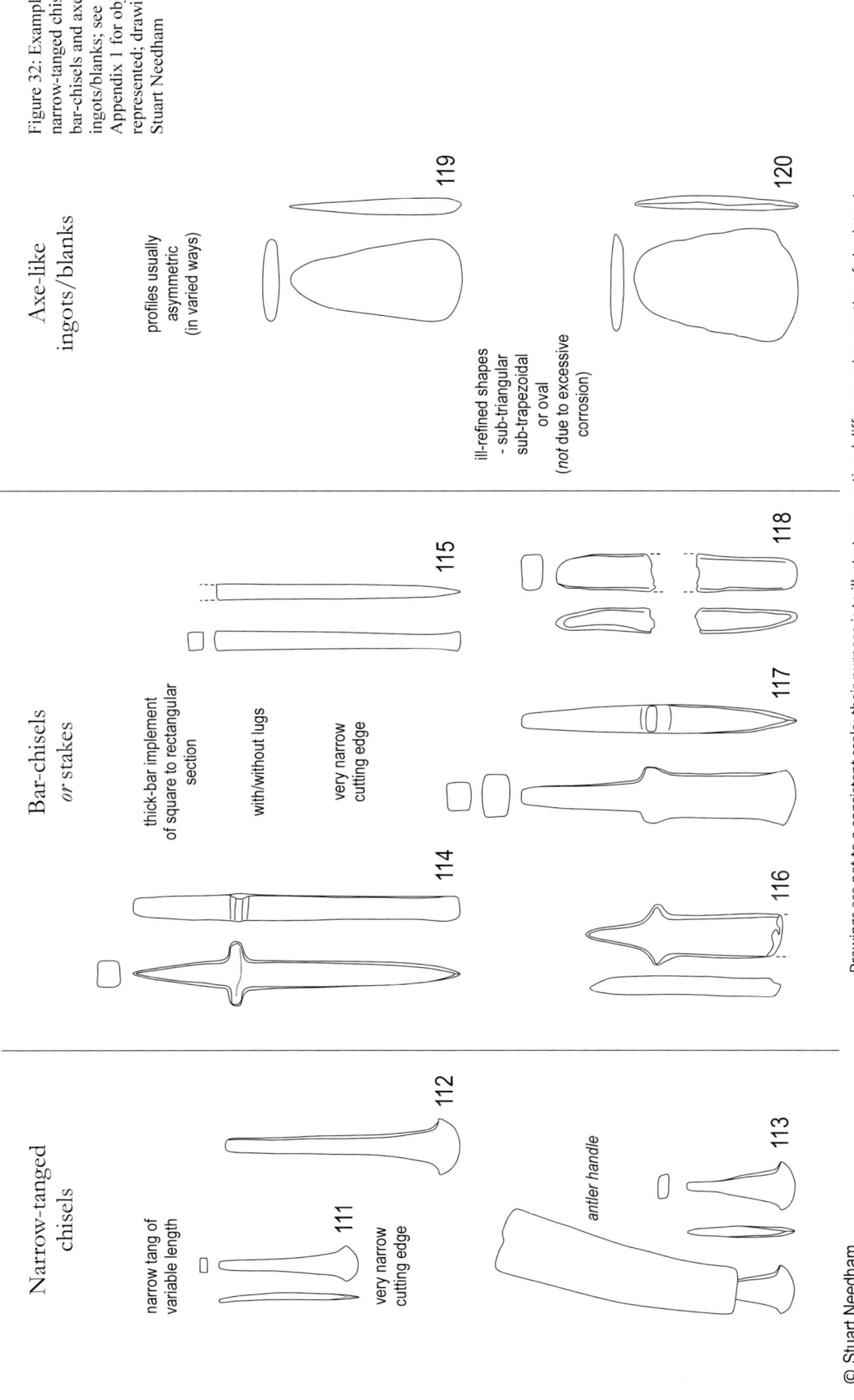

Figure 32: Examples of narrow-tanged chisels, bar-chisels and axe-like ingots/blanks; see Appendix 1 for objects represented; drawings Stuart Needham

References

Annable, F.K. & Simpson, D.D.A. 1964. *Guide Catalogue of the Neolithic and Bronze Age Collections in Devizes Museum.* Devizes: Wiltshire Archaeological and Natural History Society.

Ashbee, P. 1997. Aylesford's Bronze Age cists and burials. *Archaeologia Cantiana* 117, 147-59.

Bateman, T. 1848. *Vestiges of the Antiquities of Derbyshire, and the Sepulchral Usages of its Inhabitants from the most Remote Ages to the Reformation.* London: John Russell Smith.

Blanchet, J.-C. & Mordant, C. 1987. Les premières haches à rebords et à butée dans le basin Parisien et le Nord de la France. In J.-C. Blanchet (ed.) *Les Relations entre le Continent et les Iles Britanniques à l'Âge du Bronze: Actes du Colloques de Lille dans le cadre du 22ème Congrès préhistorique de France, 2-7 Septembre 1984*, 89-118. Amiens: Revue Archéologique de Picardie (supplementary volume).

Briard, J. 1965. *Les Dépôts Bretons et l'Age du Bronze Atlantique.* Rennes: Université de Rennes.

Britton, D. 1963. Traditions of metal-working in the later Neolithic and Early Bronze Age of Britain: part 1. *Proceedings of the Prehistoric Society* 29, 258-325.

Britton, D. 1979. The bronze axe from Mount Pleasant: description, composition and affinities. In G. Wainwright, *Mount Pleasant, Dorset: Excavations 1970-1971*, 128-38. London: Society of Antiquaries of London.

Burgess, C.B. & Cowen, J.D. 1972. The Ebnal hoard and Early Bronze Age metal-working traditions. In F. Lynch & C.B. Burgess (eds.) *Prehistoric Man in Wales and the West: Essays in Honour of Lily F. Chitty*, 167-88. Bath: Adams & Dart.

Burgess, C.B. & Richardson, C. 1985. Unpublished axes in Carlisle Museum. *Transactions of the Cumberland and Westmorland Antiquarian and Archaeological Society* 85, 43-52.

Butler, J. J. 1963. Bronze Age connections across the North Sea: a study in prehistoric trade and industrial relations between the British Isles, the Netherlands, north Germany and Scandinavia, *c*. 1700-700 BC. *Palaeohistoria* 9.

Case, H.J. 1970. Bevelled axes. In J. Filip (ed.) *Actes du VIIe Congrés International des Sciences Préhistoriques et Protohistoriques, Prague, 1966*, 657-61. Prague.

Clarke, B. 2000. A miniature flat axe or chisel from Broad Town, North Wiltshire. *Wiltshire Archaeological and Natural History Magazine* 93, 238-9.

Coffey, G. 1901. Irish copper celts. *Journal of the Anthropological Institute* 31, 265-79.

Collins, A.E.P. 1970. Bronze Age moulds in Ulster. *Ulster Journal of Archaeology* 33, 23-36.

Colquhoun, I. 1978. Bronze Age metalwork in Somerset: a catalogue of stray finds. *Proceedings of the Somerset Archaeological and Natural History Society* 122, 83-101.

Cowie, T. 1977. Dalry, Carwinning Hill. *Discovery and Excavation in Scotland 1977.*

Crawford, O.G.S. 1912. The distribution of Early Bronze Age settlements in Britain. *Geographical Journal* 40, 184-203 & 304-17.

Davey, P.J. 1973. Bronze Age metalwork in Lincolnshire. *Archaeologia* 104, 51-127.

Dobson, D.P. 1931. *The Archaeology of Somerset.* London: Methuen.

Ferrier, J. & Roussot-Larroque, J. 1971. Poignard et haches plates de Vendée. *Bulletin de la Société Préhistorique Française* 68, 83-8.

Forde-Johnston, J. 1962. A hoard of flat axes from Moel Arthur, Flintshire. *Journal of the Flintshire Historical Society* 21, 99-100.

Fox, C. 1923. *The Archaeology of the Cambridge Region.* Cambridge: University Press.

Gerloff, S. 1975. *The Early Bronze Age Daggers in Great Britain, and a reconsideration of the Wessex Culture.* Munich: Prähistorische Bronzefunde VI, 2.

Grinsell, L.V. 1968. *Guide Catalogue to the South Western British Collections.* Bristol: City Museum.

Gwilt, A. & Lewis, M. 2015. An Early Bronze Age hoard from Llanover Community, Monmouthshire. Unpublished report (Treasure case 14.25 Wales). Cardiff: Amgueddfa Cymru-National Museum Wales.

Gwilt, A., Lodwick, M., Sell, S., Koppe, J. and Davis, M. 2015. An Early Bronze Age hoard from Coity Higher Community, Bridgend. Unpublished report (Treasure case 15.12 Wales). Cardiff: Amgueddfa Cymru-National Museum Wales.

Harbison, P. 1969. *The Axes of the Early Bronze Age in Ireland.* Munich: Prähistorische Bronzefunde IX, 1.

Hart, C. 1967. *Archaeology in Dean.* Gloucester.

Hawkes, C.F.C. & Smith, M.A. 1955. *Bronze Age hoards in the British Museum.* Inventaria Archaeologica GB. 9-13. London: British Museum.

Heathcote, J.P. 1930. Excavations at barrows on Stanton Moor. *Derbyshire Archaeological Journal* 51, 1-44.

Jewitt, L.L. 1864. Bronze celts from Highlow, belonging to his Grace the Duke of Devonshire. *The Reliquary* 4, 63-4.

Kibbert, K. 1980. *Die Äxte und Beile im Mittleren Westdeutschland I.* Munich: Prähistorische Bronzefunde IX, 10.

Kinnes, I.A. 1985. *Beaker and Early Bronze Age Grave Groups.* British Bronze Age Metalwork, Associated Finds Series, A7–16. London: British Museum Publications.

Kinnes, I.A., Needham, S.P., Craddock, P.T. & Lang, J. 1979. Tin-plating in the Early Bronze Age: the Barton Stacey axe. *Antiquity* 53, 141-3.

Lawson, A.J. 1980. The Horning hoard. *Norfolk Archaeology* 37, 333-8.

Longworth, I.H. 1984. *Collared Urns of the Bronze Age in Great Britain and Ireland*. Cambridge: Cambridge University Press.

Lynch, F. 1991. *Prehistoric Anglesey: the Archaeology of the Island to the Roman Conquest*. Llangefni: Anglesey Antiquarian Society (2nd edition).

Martin, E., Plouviez, J. & Row, H. 1981. Archaeology in Suffolk: archaeological finds, 1980. *Proceedings of the Suffolk Institute of Archaeology and History* 35, 73-6.

Megaw, B.R.S. & Hardy, E.M. 1938. British decorated axes and their diffusion during the earlier part of the Bronze Age. *Proceedings of the Prehistoric Society* 4, 272–307.

Moore, C.N. & Rowlands, M. 1972. *Bronze Age Metalwork in Salisbury Museum*. Salisbury: Salisbury and South Wiltshire Museum.

Müller-Karpe, H. 1974. *Handbuch der Vorgeschichte, Band 3: Kupferzeit*. Munich: Beck.

Needham, S.P. 1979. The extent of foreign influence on Early Bronze Age axe development in southern Britain. In M. Ryan (ed.) *The Origins of Metallurgy in Atlantic Europe: Proceedings of the Fifth Atlantic Colloquium, Dublin, 1978*, 265-93. Dublin: Stationery Office.

Needham, S.P. 1983. The Early Bronze Age axeheads of central and southern England. Cardiff. Unpublished Doctoral Thesis.

Needham, S.P. 1987a. The bronzes and their implications. In A.C.H. Olivier, Excavations of a Bronze Age funerary cairn at Manor Farm, near Borwick, North Lancashire. *Proceedings of the Prehistoric Society* 53, 129-86.

Needham, S.P. 1987b. The Bronze Age. In J. Bird & D.G. Bird (eds.) *The Archaeology of Surrey to 1540*, 97-137. Guildford: Surrey Archaeological Society.

Needham, S.P. 1988. Selective deposition in the British Early Bronze Age. *World Archaeology* 20, 229-48.

Needham, S.P. 1996. Chronology and periodisation in the British Bronze Age. In K. Randsborg (ed.) *Absolute Chronology: Archaeological Europe 2500-500 BC*, 121-40. Acta Archaeologica 67.

Needham, S.P. 2004. Migdale-Marnoch: sunburst of Scottish metallurgy. In I.A. Shepherd & G.J. Barclay (eds.) *Scotland in Ancient Europe: The Neolithic and Early Bronze Age of Scotland in their European Context*, 217-45. Edinburgh: Society of Antiquaries of Scotland.

Needham, S.P. 2007. Bronze makes a Bronze Age? Considering the systemics of Bronze Age metal use and the implications of selective deposition. In C. Burgess, P. Topping & F. Lynch (eds.) *Beyond Stonehenge: Essays in Honour of Colin Burgess*, 278-87. Oxford: Oxbow.

Needham, S. 2013. Low-flanged Early Bronze Age axe. In S. Willis, *The Roman Roadside Settlement and Multi-Period Ritual Complex at Nettleton and Rothwell, Lincolnshire, Volume 1*, 162-7. Canterbury: University of Kent.

Needham, S.P. & Saville, A. 1981. Two Early Bronze Age flat axeheads from Oddington. *Transactions of the Bristol and Gloucestershire Archaeological Society* 99, 15-9.

Needham, S.P., Lawson, A.J. & Green, H.S. 1985. *Early Bronze Age Hoards.* British Bronze Age Metalwork, Associated Finds Series A1-6. London: British Museum Publications.

Needham, S., Parker Pearson, M., Tyler, A., Richards, M. & Jay, M. 2010. A first 'Wessex 1' date from Wessex. *Antiquity* 84, 363-73.

Needham, S., Davis, M., Gwilt, A., Lodwick, M., Parkes, P. and Reavill, P. 2015. A hafted halberd excavated at Trecastell, Powys: from undercurrent to uptake – the emergence and contextualisation of halberds in Wales and north-west Europe. *Proceedings of the Prehistoric Society* 81, 1-41.

Needham, S., Kenny, J., Cole, G., Montgomery, J., Jay, M., Davis, M. & Marshall, P. 2017. Death by combat at the dawn of the Bronze Age? Profiling the dagger-accompanied burial from Racton, West Sussex. *Antiquaries Journal* 97, 1-53.

Norfolk Museum Service 1977. *Bronze Age Metalwork in Norwich Castle Museum* (2nd ed.). Norwich: Norfolk Museums Service.

O'Connor, B. 2010. From Dorchester to Dieskau – some aspects of relations between Britain and central Europe during the Early Bronze Age. In H. Meller & F. Bertemes (eds.) *Der Griff nach den Sternen: Internationales Symposium in Halle (Saale) 16.-21. Februar 2005*, 591-602. Halle: Tagungen des Landesmuseums für Vorgeschichte.

O'Connor, B. & Cowie, T. 2001. Scottish connections: some recent finds of Early Bronze Age decorated axes from Scotland. In W.H. Metz, B.L. van Beek and H. Steegstra (eds.) *Patina: Essays presented to Jay Jordan Butler on the Occasion of his 80th Birthday*, 207-30. Groningen/Amsterdam.

O'Kelly, M.J. & Shell, C.A. 1979. Stone objects and a bronze axe from Newgrange, Co. Meath. In M. Ryan (ed.) *The Origins of Metallurgy in Atlantic Europe: Proceedings of the Fifth Atlantic Colloquium, Dublin, 1978*, 127-44. Dublin: Stationery Office.

Pennington, R. 1877. *Notes on the Barrows and Bone-Caves of Derbyshire (with an account of the descent into Elden Hole)*. London.

Phillip, W. 1893. Note on bronze celts found at Asterton Prolimoor. *Shropshire Notes and Queries* (Feb 17 1893), 26.

Piggott, S. 1963. Abercromby and after: the Beaker cultures of Britain re-examined. In I.Ll. Foster & L. Alcock (eds.) *Culture and Environment: Essays in honour of Sir Cyril Fox*, 53-91. London: Routledge & Kegan Paul.

Rowlands, M.J. 1976. *The Production and Distribution of Metalwork in the Middle Bronze Age of Southern Britain*. Oxford: British Archaeological Reports, British Series 31.

Rutland, R.A. & Coghlan, H.H. 1972. Bronze Age flat axes from Berkshire. *Berkshire Archaeological Journal* 66, 45-59.

Saunders, P.R. 1975-6. A flat axe from Figheldean or Netheravon. *Wiltshire Archaeological Magazine* 70/71, 125-6.

Savory, H.N. 1980. *Guide Catalogue of the Bronze Age Collections*. Cardiff: National Museum of Wales.

Schmidt, P.K. & Burgess, C.B. 1981. *The Axes of Scotland and Northern England*. Munich: Prähistorische Bronzefunde IX, 7.

Sherwin, G.A. 1942. A second bronze hoard of Arreton type found in the Isle of Wight. *Antiquaries Journal* 22, 198-201.

Smirke, E. 1865. Notice of two golden ornaments found near Padstow and communicated to the Institute by favour of H.R.H. the Prince of Wales, K.G. *Archaeological Journal* 22, 275-7.

Smirke, E. 1866-7. Observations on the gold gorgets or lunettes found near Padstow, and now in the museum at Truro. *Journal of the Royal Institute of Cornwall* 2, 134-42.

Smith, M.A. 1959. Some Somerset hoards and their place in the Bronze Age of southern Britain. *Proceedings of the Prehistoric Society* 25, 144-87.

Sprockhoff, E. 1941. Niedersachsens Bedeutung für die Bronzezeit Westeuropas. *Berichte der Römisch-Germanischen Kommission* 31 (2), 1-138.

Thomas, N. 1972. An Early Bronze Age stone axe-mould from the Walleybourne below Longden Common, Shropshire. In F. Lynch and C. Burgess (eds.) *Prehistoric Man in Wales and the West: Essays in Honour of Lily Chitty*, 161-6. Bath: Adams & Dart.

Vandkilde, H. 1996. *From Stone to Bronze: the Metalwork of the Late Neolithic and Earliest Bronze Age in Denmark*. Aarhus: Jutland Archaeological Society.

Vandkilde, H. 2017. *The Metal Hoard from Pile in Scania, Sweden: Place, Things, Time, Metals, and Worlds around 2000 BCE*. Aarhus University Press.

Von Brunn, W.A. 1959. *Die Hortfunde der Frühen Bronzezeit ins Sachsen-Anhalt, Sachsen und Thuringen*. Berlin.

Watkin, J.R. 1987. Three finds of Bronze Age metalwork from the Vale of York. *Proceedings of the Prehistoric Society* 53, 493-8.

West, A. 2014. A strange and unusual Early Bronze Age axe from Norfolk. *Later Prehistoric Finds Group Newsletter* no 3 (June 2014), 16-8.

Yates, M.J. 1979. The discovery of two flat bronze axes near Caerlaverock Castle, Dumfries. *Transactions of the Dumfries and Galloway Natural History and Antiquarian Society* 54, 147-9.

Appendix 1: Objects represented in the type series of Chalcolithic and Early Bronze Age axes and chisels (Figs 17 – 32)

Implements are not shown at a consistent scale; their purpose is to illustrate proportional differences irrespective of absolute size. Formal decoration – both punched stroke and hammer-fluted – is omitted, but 'structural' faceting of the sides is shown, as are bevels on the faces.

Most museum accession numbers are as encountered at the time of study. Fuller details can be obtained from the references cited; the purpose here is only to reference the immediate source of the illustration; the vast majority have been drawn from the object by the author.

No	Classification	Provenance	Collection & accession no	Illustration source (redrawn from)	Notes
1	1A Minto	Moel Arthur, Nannerch/Cilcain, Flintshire	Manchester University Museum, 34687	Forde-Johnston 1962, 100 fig 1.3	
2	1A Minto	Farncombe, Surrey (?)	Charterhouse School Museum, 167-1957	Needham 1983, Sy 4/1	some doubt as to the validity of the provenance
3	1A Minto	No provenance	Museum of London 0.1168	Needham 1983, UP 24	ex-Layton collection and possibly from the Thames
4	2A Burley Camp	Burley Camp, Bridestowe, Devon	Plymouth Museum, 379	Needham 1983, Dv 1	
5	2A Burley Camp	Moel Arthur, Nannerch/Cilcain, Flintshire	Manchester University Museum, 34686	Forde-Johnston 1962, 100 fig 1.1	
6	2A Burley Camp	No provenance	Dorchester Museum, 1884.9.9	Needham 1983, UP 12	
7	2B Lode	Bottisham Lode, Lode, Cambridgeshire	Cambridge University Museum, 91.14	Needham 1983, Ca 30	
8	2B Lode	Summer Hill, The Malverns, Worcestershire	Private ownership	PAS: HESH-84D8A5 (photograph)	
9	2B Lode	Suffolk	Ipswich Museum, 1920.51.1	Needham 1983, Sf 31	
10	2C Purdis Farm	Bucklesham Road, Purdis Farm, Suffolk	Ipswich Museum, 959-162	Needham 1983, Sf 27	surface has been stripped since original study
11	2C Purdis Farm	Uphill allotments, Weston-super-Mare, Avon	Weston-super-Mare Museum, 63/246	Needham 1983, Av 9	
12	2C Purdis Farm	Thruxton Hill, Thruxton, Hampshire	Private ownership	Needham 1983, Ha 15	
13	2C Ironbridge	River Severn, Ironbridge, Shropshire	Shrewsbury Museum, SHYMS: A/2003/028	Needham 1983, Sp 10	
14	2C Ironbridge	Chapel Fields, St Margarets, (probably) Hounslow, Greater London	British Museum, 1891,0514.60	Needham 1983, GL 3	alternatively from Stanstead St Margarets, Hertfordshire
15	2D Halberton	Rowridge Farm, Halberton, Devon	Exeter Museum, 1936/38 (loan)	Needham 1983, Dv 5	
16	2D Halberton	Penolva, Paul, Cornwall	Penzance Museum, 84/42	Needham 1983, Cw 5	surface probably eroded

17	2D Halberton	Harpley Common, Harpley, Norfolk	Private ownership	Needham 1983, Nf 21	
18	2D Halberton	The Hough, Malpas, Cheshire	Private ownership	PAS LVPL93 (photograph)	
19	2D Halberton	Jordan Hill, Weymouth, Dorset	Dorchester Museum, 1885.16.2	Needham 1983, Ds 9	diminutive example
20	2E *hachette*	Upper Viney, Blakeney Gloucestershire	Private ownership	Needham et al. 1996	
21	2E *hachette*	Horning, Norfolk	Private ownership	Lawson 1980, 336 fig 5 no 6	
22	3A Scunthorpe	Morecambe Avenue, Scunthorpe, N Lincolnshire	Scunthorpe Museum	Needham 1983, Hb 9	
23	3A Scunthorpe	Millfield, Harthill Stanton, Derbyshire	Sheffield Museum, J.93-476	Needham 1983, Dy 6	
24	3A Lansdown	Lansdown, Charlcombe, Avon	British Museum, 1964,1206.11	Needham 1983, Av 8	
25	3A Lansdown *waisted variant*	Yaxley Fen, Yaxley, Cambridgeshire	British Museum, 1882,0621.2	Needham 1983, Ca 44	
26	3B Boreland	Ynys, Talwrn, Llanddyfnan, Anglesey	Private ownership	Lynch 1991, fig 58	large axe
27	3B Boreland	River Thames at Bray, Berkshire/Buckinghamshire	Reading Museum, 44:52	Needham 1983, BB 2	
28	3B Boreland	Boreland, Low Glenstockdale, Dumfries & Galloway	Stranraer Museum, 1964-8	Needham 1983, 284 fig 11.2 (lower)	large axe
29	3C Harlyn Bay	Raglan, Llanarth Community, Monmouthsire	Private ownership	Lodwick NMWPA 2013.146 (photograph)	
30	3C Harlyn Bay	Harlyn Bay, St Merryn, Cornwall	Truro Museum	Needham 1983, Cw 10/1	
31	3C Harlyn Bay	Littleport, Cambridgeshire	British Museum, WG 1793	Needham 1983, Ca 28	axe in two halves
32	3D Barton Stacey	Pennard Community, Swansea	Swansea Museum	PAS: NMGW-89E573	
33	3D Barton Stacey	Barton Stacey, Hampshire	British Museum, 1979,0602.1	Needham 1983, Ha 3	
34	3D Barton Stacey	Common Road, Stotfold, Bedfordshire	Private ownership	Needham 1983, Bd 1	
35	3E Brithdir	Brithdir/Pont Caradog, Caerphilly	Ashmolean Museum, 1927.2370	Needham 1979, 283 fig 10 (upper right)	
36	3E Brithdir	Brithdir/Pont Caradog, Caerphilly	British Museum, WG 1801	Needham 1979, 283 fig 10 (lower left)	
37	3E Brithdir	Thornes Farm (near), Oddington, Gloucestershire	Cheltenham Museum, 1980:2182	Needham 1983, Gs 5/2	
38	3E Brithdir	River Thames at Battersea, Greater	British Museum, 1906,0702.1	Needham 1983, GL 8	large axe

		London			
39	3E/3F borderline	Castle Rising, Norfolk	British Museum, 1866,0627.10	Needham 1983, Nf 9/1	
40	3F Moot Low	Moot Low Barrow, Newton Grange, Derbyshire	Sheffield Museum, J.93-477	Needham 1983, Dy 12/1	
41	3F Moot Low	Clipsall Field, Soham, Cambridgeshire	Cambridge University Museum, 71.49	Needham 1983, Ca 36	
42	3F Moot Low	Oxwich Bay, Penrice, Swansea	Swansea Museum	personal study	axe in two halves; large axe
43	3F Moot Low	St Bertram's Well, Ilam, Staffordshire	Ashmolean Museum, N.C.337	Needham 1983, Sd 2	large axe
44	3G Knapton	Newport Railway Station (near), Newport	Ashmolean Museum, 1927.2368	Needham 1979, 286 fig 12.1 (right)	
45	3G Knapton	'Near the Tower' (?River Thames), Tower Hamlets, Greater London	British Museum, 1875,0401.4	Needham 1983, GL 22	
46	3G Knapton	Knapton, East Yorkshire	British Museum, WG 1810	personal study	
47	3G Knapton	Methwold Hythe, Methwold, Norfolk	Cambridge University Museum, Z.4297	Needham 1983, Nf 38	
48	4A Kettering	Kettering, Northamptonshire	British Museum, WG 1792	Needham 1983, Np 2	
49	4A Kettering	Brithdir/Pont Caradog, Caerphilly	British Museum, WG 1802	Needham 1979, 283 fig 10 (upper left)	
50	4A Kettering	Shuttlestone Plantation, Parwich Moor, Parwich, Derbyshire	Sheffield Museum, J.93-473	Needham 1983, Dy 13/1	
51	4B Aylesford	Newport Railway Station (near), Newport	Ashmolean Museum, 1927.2369	Needham 1979, 286 fig 12.1 (left)	
52	4B Aylesford	Rye Close, Mile Cross, Norwich, Norfolk	Norwich Museum, 147.982(2)	Needham 1983, Nf 45/2	
53	4B Aylesford	Parish Field Gravel Pit, Aylesford, Kent	Maidstone Museum	Needham 1983, Kt 2/1	large axe
54	4B Aylesford	Near Dhustone Quarry, Bitterley Shropshire	Shrewsbury Museum, SHYMS: A/2003/205	Needham 1983, Sp 3/1	large axe
55	4C Mount Pleasant	Long Wittenham Weir (near), Appleford(?), Oxfordshire	Ashmolean Museum, PR.371	Needham 1983, Ox 1	
56	4C Mount Pleasant	Mount Pleasant, West Stafford, Dorset	Dorchester Museum	Needham 1983, Ds 8	
57	4C Mount Pleasant	Sully Community, Vale of Glamorgan	Private ownership	Lodwick & Gwilt 2011	
58	4D Cardiff Castle	Stow-cum-Quy, Cambridgeshire	Cambridge University Museum, 83.114	Needham 1983, Ca 38	
59	4D Cardiff Castle	Wold Farm, Willerby, North	British Museum, WG 1807	Needham 1979, 287 fig 13	

				(upper left)	
		Yorkshire	Amgueddfa Cymru - National Museum Wales, 57.514	Needham 1983, fig 37.1	
60	4D Cardiff Castle	Cardiff Castle, Cardiff			
61	4E Glebe Farm	Glebe Farm, Winterbourne Steepleton, Dorset	Dorchester Museum, 1892.30.1	Needham 1983, Ds 14	
62	4E Glebe Farm(?)	Moorwell Road, Yaddlethorpe, Bottesford, North Lincolnshire	Scunthorpe Museum, 124.58	Needham 1983, Hb 2	surfaces all reduced; conceivably an eroded Class 5A axe
63	4E Whittington	Whittington, Gloucestershire	Society of Antiquaries of London collection	Needham 1983, Gs 8	
64	4E Whittington	Isleham, Cambridgeshire	Mildenhall Museum (since gone missing)	Needham 1983, Ca 25	
65	4E Whittington	Yorkshire	British Museum, 1853,1115.9	Needham 1983, fig 40.2	large axe
66	4E Whittington	Nettleton, Lincolnshire	Lincoln Museum, 175.98	Needham 2013	
67	4E Whittington	North Rauceby, Lincolnshire	Boston Museum	Needham 1983, Li 7	
68	4E Whittington *sinuous variant*	Suffolk (?)	Ashmolean Museum, 1927.2372	Needham 1983, Sf 32	
69	4E Whittington *sinuous variant*	?Netherwood Manor, Thornbury, Herefordshire	Hereford Museum, 6743/1	Needham 1983, HW 3/1	some doubt as to the validity of the provenance
70	4F Asterton Prolley Moor	Asterton Prolley Moor, Myndtown, Shropshire	Shrewsbury Museum, (previously B.4)	Needham 1983, Sp 8/1	
71	4F Asterton Prolley Moor	Castle Bryn Amlwg, Bettws-y-Crwyn, Shropshire	Welshpool Museum	Needham 1983, Sp 2/1	
72	4F Asterton Prolley Moor	Breach Farm, Llanbleddian, Vale of Glamorgan	Amgueddfa Cymru - National Museum Wales, 38.37.1	Needham 1988, 238 fig 4.2	diminutive example
73	4F Asterton Prolley Moor	Bush Barrow, Wilsford G5, Wilsford-cum-Lake, Wiltshire	Devizes Museum, 747	Needham 1988, 238 fig 4.3	
74	5A Horncastle	Near Horncastle, Lincolnshire	British Museum, WG 1813	Needham 1983, Li 4	
75	5A Horncastle	Redbourne, North Lincolnshire	York Museum	Needham 1983, Hb 6	
76	5A Horncastle	Reading (near), Berkshire	Reading Museum, 14:68	Needham 1983, Br 3	
77	5A Horncastle	Moon's Hill, Totland, Isle of Wight	Carisbrooke Museum	Needham 1983, IW 3/4	
78	5B Ashford	Ashford golf links, Ashford, Kent	Maidstone Museum, 55.1949	Needham 1983, Kt 1	
79	5B Ashford	Bridgham, Norfolk	Cambridge University Museum, 1920.807	Needham 1983, Nf 5	diminutive example
80	5B Greengate	'Deran', Greengate, Swanton Morley, Norfolk	Private ownership	Needham 1983, Nf 52	diminutive example
81	5B Maidenhead	Norfolk	Norwich Museum, 76.94(753)	Needham 1983, Nf 58	
82	5C Bisham	Moon's Hill, Totland, Isle of Wight	Carisbrooke Museum	Needham 1983, IW 3/2	

83	5C Bisham	River Thames at Bisham, Berkshire/Buckinghamshire	British Museum, 1893,1219.1	Needham 1983, BB 1	
84	5C Bisham	Stonehenge Bottom, Amesbury, Wiltshire	Salisbury Museum, 33/53 (loan)	Needham 1983, Wi 3	
85	5D West Drayton	Blackdyke Farm, Hockwold-cum-Wilton, Norfolk	Private ownership	Needham 1983, Nf 27/1	
86	5D West Drayton	West Drayton Railway Station, Yiewsley and West Drayton, Greater London	British Museum, 1933,0406.124	Needham 1983, GL 23	
87	5D West Drayton	White Horse Hill, Osmington, Dorset	British Museum, 1875,0401.6	Needham 1983, Ds 5	
88	5D West Drayton *swollen variant*	Poslingford Hall, Poslingford, Suffolk	British Museum, 1845,0510.4	Needham 1983, Sf 26/4	
89	5D West Drayton *waisted variant*	Arreton Down, Arreton, Isle of Wight	British Museum, 1985,0302.1	Needham 1983, IW 1/3	
90	5D Staunton	Staunton, Gloucestershire	Ashmolean Museum, 1927.2580	Needham 1983, Gs 7	
91	5D Staunton	Grunty Fen, Wilburton, Cambridgeshire	Alnwick Castle Museum, 1880.197	Needham 1983, Ca 43/1	
92	5D Staunton	Queensway, Wellingborough, Northamptonshire	Kettering Museum, 1967.26	Needham 1983, Np 3	diminutive example
93	5E Clifton	Clifton, Nottinghamshire	Nottingham Museum	Needham 1983, Ng 8	
94	5E Clifton	Rocky Parks Field, Plymstock, Devon	British Museum, 1869,1220.6	Needham 1983, Dv 8/6	
95	5E (cf 5B)	Rocky Parks Field, Plymstock, Devon	British Museum, 1869,1220.12	Needham 1983, Dv 8/12	
96	5 *Irish style*	Burwell Fen, Burwell, Cambridgeshire	Cambridge University Museum, 83.116	Needham 1983, Ca 5	
97	5 *Irish style*	The Channel off Hastings, East Sussex	Rouen Museum	Needham 1983, Sx 13	
98	3 axe-chisel	Broughton Bay, Llangenith, Llanmadoc & Cheriton Community, Swansea	Private ownership	Amgueddfa Cymru - National Museum Wales unpublished BA record sheet 97/8	
99	3 axe-chisel	Aldershot, Hampshire	Whereabouts unknown	Needham 1983, Ha 1	
100	3 axe-chisel	Kings Bromley, Staffordshire	Private ownership	drawing supplied by Richard Davis (2000)	
101	4B/C axe-chisel	Whitchurch Rural, Shropshire	Private ownership	PAS HESH-041538	
102	4B/C axe-chisel	Firle, East Sussex	Lewes Museum, B.15	Needham 1983, Sx 10	
103	4B/C axe-chisel	Gooderstone, Norfolk	Norwich Museum, 210.971	Needham 1983, Nf 18	

104	4B/C axe-chisel	Ty'n-y-pwll, Llanddyfnan, Anglesey	Amgueddfa Cymru - National Museum Wales, 42.395/5	Needham 1988, 238 fig 4.5
105	4D/E axe-chisel	Warburton, Trafford, Greater Manchester	Private ownership?	photograph supplied by Nick Herepath (2000)
106	4D/E axe-chisel	Padgbury Lane, Congleton, Cheshire	Private ownership	Needham 1983, Ch 1
107	4D/E axe-chisel	Capel Quarries, Gorslas, Llanarthney, Carmarthenshire	Amgueddfa Cymru - National Museum Wales, 29.38	Needham 1983, fig 91.2
108	4D/E axe-chisel	Hercules Road (Golf course west of), Hellesdon, Norfolk	Private ownership	Needham 1983, Nf 23
109	4D/E axe-chisel *looped variant*	Bryn Crûg, Gwynedd	Whereabouts unknown	Needham 1988, 238 fig 4.4
110	4D/E axe-chisel *perforated variant*	Chatteris Fen, Chatteris, Cambridgeshire	Cambridge University Museum, 63.177	Needham 1983, Ca 11
111	Narrow-tanged chisel	Crabtree Farmhouse (barrow N of), Froxfield, Hampshire	Hampshire Cultural Trust (ex-Winchester City Museum), 117.2	personal study
112	Narrow-tanged chisel	Ty'n-y-pwll, Llanddyfnan, Anglesey	Amgueddfa Cymru - National Museum Wales, 42.395/2	Savory 1980, 199 fig 51 no 334.2
113	Narrow-tanged chisel	Collingbourne Kingston barrow G4, Wiltshire	Devizes Museum, 670	Needham 1983, fig 92.2
114	Bar-chisel/stake	Coombe Dingle, Westbury upon Trym, Bristol, Avon	Bristol Museum, E1731	Needham 1983, Av 6/4
115	Bar-chisel/stake	Rocky Parks Field, Plymstock, Devon	British Museum, 1869,1220.13	Needham 1983, Dv 8/21
116	Bar-chisel/stake	Ebnal, Whittington, Shropshire	Whereabouts unknown	Needham 1983, Sp 11/7	illustration based on Albert Way drawings, Society of Antiquaries of London
117	Bar-chisel/stake	Balneil Farm (NE of), Dumfries & Galloway (Wigtownshire)	National Museums Scotland, EQ 342	Burgess & Cowen 1972, 174 fig 5
118	Bar-chisel/stake	Stanton Moor barrow T3, Stanton, Derbyshire	Sheffield Museum	Needham 1983, fig 92.1
119	Axe-like ingot	Llancarfan Community, Vale of Glamorgan	Private ownership	Amgueddfa Cymru - National Museum Wales unpublished BA record sheet 98/3
120	Axe-like ingot	Wallingford, Berkshire	Reading Museum, 1948:64	Needham 1983, Br 6

Appendix 2: A critical path for the classification of Chalcolithic and Early Bronze Age axes and chisels

The following sequence of yes/no questions will correctly classify the vast majority of implements. Working down from the top, whenever the answer is 'no', proceed to the next line at the same hierarchical level. The correct identification is the first emboldened text following a 'yes' answer.

- Does the implement have a very slender haft end? → ***narrow-tanged chisel***
- Does the implement have a thick bar section? → ***bar-chisel***
- Is the cutting edge narrow (RWE usually < 0.45)? → axe-chisel
  - Does it have lenticular profile? → ***Class 3 axe-chisel***
  - Does it have a lozengic profile? → Class 4 axe-chisel
    - Are the sides inflected at the stop bevel → ***Class 4B/C axe-chisel***
    - Are the sides more or less continuous? → ***Class 4D/E/F axe-chisel***

Remainder are true axes:

- Does it have high-ish flanges (RHF > 0.015) → Class 5 [*or* a Middle Bronze Age type]
  - Are the flanges low for the class (RHF < 0.025) *and* in relatively good condition? → ***Sub-class 5A Type Horncastle***
  - Is the cutting edge relatively narrow (RWE usually < 0.50)? → Sub-class 5B
    - Is the body narrow (MRW < 0.81)? → ***Sub-class 5B Type Greengate***
    - Is the body relatively chunky for the type *and* the stop feature a bump? → ***Sub-class 5B Type Maidenhead***
    - Remainder (body of moderate width) → ***Sub-class 5B Type Ashford***
  - Is the body narrow (MRW < 0.81)? → ***Sub-class 5C Type Bisham***
  - Is the body broad (MRW > 1.0)? → Sub-class 5E
    - Is the overall shape comparable to Sub-class 5B? → ***Sub-class 5E (cf 5B)***
    - Remainder (shapes comparable to 5D) → ***Sub-class 5E Type Clifton***
  - Is the body medium-broad (MRW 0.81 – 1.0)? → Sub-class 5D
    - Is the lower blade fan-shaped and the stop feature (usually) a bump? → ***Sub-class 5D Type Staunton***
    - Remainder (standard, 'crescentic' lower blade) → ***Sub-class 5D Type West Drayton (or untyped variant)***

No evidence for higher flanges → Classes 1 – 4

- Is the profile 'parallel-faced' (*not* lenticular or lozengic)? → Class 1
  - Does the shape match Irish Type Cappeen (see detailed definition above)? → ***Sub-class 1A Type Minto***
  - Remainder → ***Class 1*** (*untyped as yet*)
- Is the profile lenticular? → Classes 2 – 3

- Is the butt broad (RWB > 0.46, RWB' > 0.27)? → Class 2
  - Is the axe very squat (RWE > 0.70)? → ***Sub-class 2E hachette***
  - Does the shape match Sub-class 1A? → ***Sub-class 2A Type Burley Camp***
  - Is the shape trapezoidal with negligible or no blade-tip out-turn? → ***Sub-class 2D Type Halberton***
  - Is the butt fairly squared, the body gently expanding *and* the cutting edge shallow (RDE < 0.30) with out-turned tips? → ***Sub-class 2B Type Bottisham Lode***
  - Is the butt somewhat arched, the body gently expanding *and* the cutting edge shallow (RDE < 0.30) with out-turned tips? → Sub-class 2C
    - Is the butt and body broad (RWB 0.48 – 0.56)? → ***Sub-class 2C Type Purdis Farm***
    - Is the butt and body very broad (RWB > 0.59)? → ***Sub-class 2C Type Ironbridge***
- Is the butt less broad? → Class 3
  - Is the butt moderately broad (RWB 0.38 – 0.46) → Sub-class 3A
    - Do the sides expand in fairly straight lines? → ***Sub-class 3A Type Scunthorpe***
    - Do the sides expand little at first, but progressively swing outwards? → ***Sub-class 3A Type Lansdown***
  - Is the cutting edge very broad (RWE > 0.66)? → ***Sub-class 3B Type Boreland***
  - Is the mid-blade relatively narrow (RW3 < 0.47)? → Sub-classes 3G & 3F
    - Is the cutting edge very shallow (RDE < 0.16) *and* the haft end very slender? → ***Sub-class 3F Type Moot Low***
    - Is the cutting edge moderately deep (RDE 0.20 – 0.25) *and* the haft end moderately broad? → ***Sub-class 3G Type Knapton***
  - Do the sides expand relatively strongly in near-straight lines (EH > 0.15)? → ***Sub-class 3C Type Harlyn Bay***
  - Is the side expansion moderate (EH 0.11 – 0.15) and gently curving? → ***Sub-class 3D Type Barton Stacey***
  - Are sides more strongly curved with little expansion along the haft end (EH < 0.11)? → ***Sub-class 3E Type Brithdir***
- Is the profile lozengic (usually with stop-bevel)? → Class 4
  - Is the mid-blade broad (RW3 > 0.48)? → ***Sub-class 4A Type Kettering***
  - Is the mid-blade medium-broad (RW3 0.41 – 0.48) → Sub-classes 4B & Sub-class 4E Type Glebe Farm
    - Is side curvature more or less symmetrical (ASD < 0.65)? → ***Sub-class 4B Type Aylesford***
    - Is side curvature asymmetrical (ASD > 0.65)? → ***Sub-class 4E Type Glebe Farm***
  - Is mid-blade narrow (RW3 0.33 – 0.41)? → Sub-classes 4C, 4D & 4E Type Whittington
    - Are sides slightly angled *and* their overall curvature modest (RMO < 0.10)? → ***Sub-class 4C Type Mount Pleasant***
    - Is side curvature asymmetric (ASD > 0.65) *but* rather modest (RMO < 0.06), *and* cutting edge depth moderate to deep (RDE 0.20 – 0.34)? → ***Sub-class 4D Type Cardiff Castle***
    - Is side curvature asymmetric (ASD > 0.65) *and* strong (RMO > 0.06) → ***Sub-class 4E Type Whittington***
  - Is mid-blade very narrow (RW3 < 0.32)? → ***Sub-class 4F Type Asterton Prolley Moor***